WHY in the WORLD?

Questions! Answers! Activities!

Published by Playmore Inc., Publishers, 58 Main Street, 2nd Floor, Hackensack, N.J. 07601 and Waldman Publishing Corp., 570 Seventh Avenue, New York, N.Y. 10018

Copyright © MMV Playmore Inc., Publishers and Waldman Publishing Corp., New York, New York

The Playmore/Waldman® and Bug Logo® are registered trademarks of Playmore Inc., Publishers and Waldman Publishing Corp.,New York, New York

Printed i

W9-DIL-386

What type of creatures were dinosaurs?

Dinosaurs were reptiles, like today's lizards.

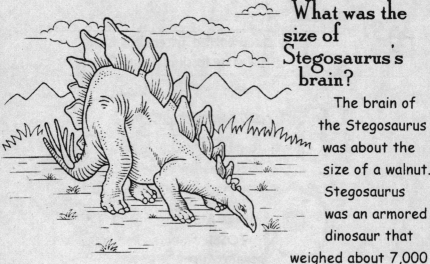

What was the size of Stegosaurus's brain?

The brain of the Stegosaurus was about the size of a walnut. Stegosaurus was an armored dinosaur that weighed about 7,000 pounds and was from 15 to 30 feet long.

What does the name "dinosaur" mean, and when was the name given to these animals?

"Dinosaur" means a "fearful or terrifying lizard." The name was coined in 1842 by Richard Owen, a British scientist.

How many horns did a Triceratops have on its head?

The Triceratops had three long and sharp horns.

What was the wingspan of a flying pterosaur?

The flying reptiles called pterosaurs had wingspans of

more than 25 feet. They were the largest flying creatures known to have existed.

Fossil Hunt Word Search

Let's go on a dinosaur hunt! Find and circle the words in the word list. Look across and down.

Word List
DINOSAUR
FOSSIL
PTEROSAURS
REPTILE

D	I	N	O	S	A	U	R	X	P
F	D	F	E	R	E	Z	X	T	T
R	Q	W	E	R	O	E	V	R	E
E	W	E	R	G	H	J	K	N	R
P	O	Z	M	P	Q	J	E	C	O
T	A	G	S	J	D	K	C	M	S
I	O	E	F	O	S	S	I	L	A
L	X	V	T	Y	K	L	A	U	U
E	K	L	J	F	G	R	A	E	R
D	G	E	F	S	P	O	R	H	S

3   Solution, see page 130.

What is the most ancient known dinosaur?

Three different dinosaurs hold the record for being the oldest known. They lived about 228 million years ago. They were all small, measuring no more than five feet in length. They all had two legs. They were Eoraptor, a dog-sized meat eater; Saturnalia, a plant eater; and Pisanosaurus, also a plant eater.

What is the smallest known dinosaur?

One candidate for the smallest dinosaur is Compsognathus, a small predator that weighed about six pounds. It was about the same size as a modern-day chicken. Compsognathus means "pretty jaw."

Very small dinosaur fossils are hard to find, because the bones of small dinosaurs were easily destroyed. Tiny dinosaurs were often gulped down whole by larger dinosaurs, leaving no traces of them.

Could dinosaurs have survived into modern times?

No surviving dinosaurs have been found. According to scientists, it is not likely that any dinosaurs will ever be found alive and thriving in some far-off part of the globe.

FAST FACT

Most dinosaurs were not smart and had the IQ of a turtle or a lizard.

Did meat-eating dinosaurs replace lost teeth like sharks do?

Unlike mammals, meat-eating dinosaurs regularly lost and replaced their teeth.

Did any dinosaurs live entirely in water?

No dinosaur lived entirely in water. There were no known plant-eating dinosaurs that were like today's dugongs or manatees. Even fish-eating dinosaurs did not stay too long in the water because of the presence of crocodiles that were 50 feet long. Plant-eating sauropods may have taken an occasional dip to cool off if there weren't any enemies in the water.

Dino Bite!

This dinosaur has lost 12 of his teeth. They are scattered in this picture. Can you find them all? We've circled one to help you.

Solution, see page 130.

What is the largest reptile?

The saltwater, or estuarine, crocodile is the world's largest reptile. It can reach 26 feet in length and weigh more than 2,000 pounds. This species lives in the coastal waters of India, southern China, and Malaysia. It has been known to attack humans.

Is the sea turtle born in the sea?

No, it's born ashore on a beach. After hatching, the baby sea turtle has to crawl, sometimes for several days, to get to the ocean. He has to do this while dodging seagulls that like to eat baby turtles.

How do alligators communicate with other alligators?

Alligators use grunts, bellows, and hisses to communicate with one another and to threaten other creatures.

How do black-necked cobras attack their enemies?

Black-necked, or spitting, cobras can spit venom into the eyes of enemies up to eight feet away.

FAST FACT

The ten-foot-long Komodo dragon is the world's largest lizard. It can live for up to 100 years.

Reptilian Fill-ins

Insert a different letter of the alphabet into each of the five empty spaces to form the name of a different reptile. Each reptile's name has five or more letters reading across. We've started off the puzzle with the first answer, turtle.

Q	T	U	R	T	L	E	V	U	P	S
R	X	P	S	N		K	E	L	A	D
Y	A	L	L	I		A	T	O	R	F
T	V	N	C	G		C	K	O	F	S
L	B	C	L	I		A	R	D	W	K
O	M	B	R	A	T	L	E	R	O

7   Solution, see page 131.

How do birds fly?

The bird has powerful chest muscles that move its wings up and down, pushing air down and lifting the bird up.

Why can't all birds fly?

If a bird doesn't have the very strong chest muscles that let it flap its wings, it'll never get off the ground. That's why the ostrich, emu, and penguin can't fly. But they make up for it. The ostrich and emu run very fast. And the penguin is a very strong swimmer, using its wings as fins.

Penguin

How can the hummingbird fly backward?

Because the beautiful hummingbird is so small and its wings beat so fast, it can fly in ways no other bird can. It can fly backward, and it can hover in the air, not moving at all. It's the helicopter of the bird world! It's called a hummingbird because its strong wing beat is so rapid that it produces a hum.

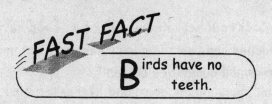

B irds have no teeth.

Why do birds sing?

A bird has a special voice box, or syrinx, that lets it sing a beautiful song. This song lets other birds know who's in the neighborhood. Each bird has a song that's special to its own species, so a pigeon's sweet coo could never be mistaken for a robin's cheerful warble. If the bird is raised in a cage and never hears its own kind, it will still be able to sing its special song, but it will be a very simple melody, and not as varied as if it had learned from its parents and other birds.

Mixed-up Birds

Somebody has mixed up all these birds. It's up to you to straighten out the mess and give the birds their right names.

meadow eagle   1._____ eagle

bald owl   2._____ owl

hoot warbler   3._____ warbler

yellow-bellied lark   4._____ lark

fly-catching sapsucker   5._____ sapsucker

Solution, see page 131.

How do cockroaches know there's food around?

Cockroaches can use their very sensitive antennae to detect very small quantities of food.

What do fireflies eat?

Young fireflies, or glowworms, eat snails and worms. They eat at night. Adult fireflies may eat nectar or nothing at all.

Aside from flies, are there any other insects with just one set of wings?

Of the major insect groups, flies are the only ones who have just one pair of wings.

FAST FACT

Moths generally have thicker bodies than butterflies, and they rest with their wings outstretched or folded, while butterflies place their wings back to back when resting.

How do bees know where there are flowers around?

They dance! When a worker bee finds a source of nectar, it tells the other bees how far and where the flowers are. All this is told through a dance that is done in the hive.

Can woolly bears predict the weather?

Woolly bears are the beautifully striped hairy caterpillars of tiger moths. And they don't know any more about the weather than humans do. It's a fable.

Can crickets tell you what the temperature is?

Yes! The higher the temperature, the faster the chirping. Just add 40 to the number of chirps you hear in 15 seconds and you'll know what the approximate temperature is in degrees Fahrenheit.

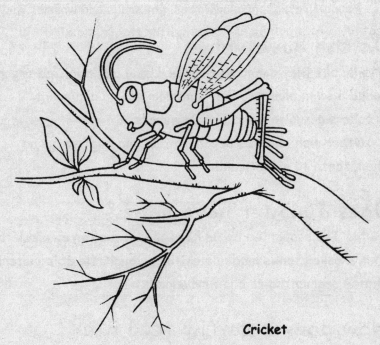

Cricket

Changeable Insects

Change the first insect name into the second insect name by changing only one letter at a time. Here is an example: Go from "Moth" to "Wasp": MOTH GOTH GOSH GASH GASP WASP.

BEE   ANT
BUG   FLY

Solution, see page 131.

Do flying fish really fly?

Using its fins as wings, the flying fish can take off from the water at a speed of 35 miles per hour. It can stay in the air for up to 15 seconds. It will fly as high as 36 feet up and glide along for about 200 yards.

Do fish have voices?

No, but they can make sounds. Using a specialized organ called a swim bladder, fish can boom, drum, and grunt. Croakers actually sound like drummers.

Other fish, such as ocean sunfish and hogfish, grind their teeth to make sounds.

Does a lobster have bones?

No. It's supported by its hard shell, called an exoskeleton. The exoskeleton is made of chitin, a tough, flexible material that is segmented to allow movement.

How does a starfish feed itself?

It can eat small animals whole but deals with larger prey by turning its stomach inside out onto the prey, and then digesting it.

What keeps seals and sea lions warm?

A layer of fatty tissue called blubber, sometimes as thick as 20 inches, lies just under the inner layer of skin to keep seals, sea lions, walruses, and whales warm in cold temperatures.

Why does a catfish have whiskers?

A catfish's whiskers, or barbels, are organs of touch and taste, and help the fish find food.

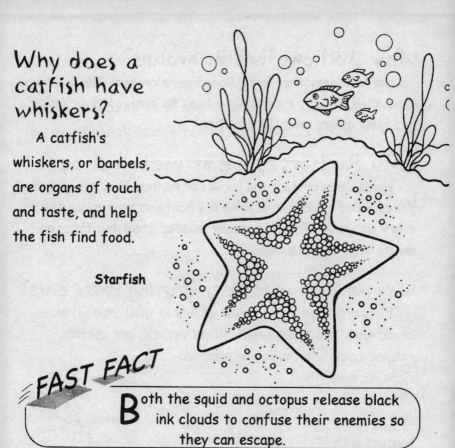

Starfish

FAST FACT

Both the squid and octopus release black ink clouds to confuse their enemies so they can escape.

Catch the Fish

There are five fish hiding in the sentences below. Each one reads across two words. The first fish, SALMON, is underlined for you. Can you spot the other four?

1. Because of the ATM's refu<u>sal, mon</u>ey couldn't be with drawn.
2. "Take your vitamin now," the doctor ordered.
3. When you finish, Arkansas should be your last stop.
4. "Hail, Caesar, dine with us," invited the Roman restaurant owner.
5. In Madagascar, peanuts are an important crop.

13

Solution, see page 131.

Why do lions live in groups?

Unlike most other cats, lions live in groups. These groups are called prides. Prides allow lions to protect their young and hunt larger animals together.

Why do horses wear metal shoes?

Horseshoes protect the hooves of horses. They are U-shaped plates nailed to the rim of a horse's hoof and are replaced about every six weeks. They are usually made of steel, but today aluminum or plastic may be used.

Why do elephants keep flapping their ears?

Elephants don't have sweat glands in their skin. Their broad ears, which have many blood vessels, are used to release body heat. When an elephant flaps its ears, the blood vessels come in contact with the air, cooling the elephant's blood.

Elephant

Why do beavers build dams?

Beavers build their homes below the water level of the ponds, lakes, or rivers in which they live. Strong swimmers, they enter and leave these underwater homes (lodges) secretly, so their enemies won't catch them. The watertight dams the beavers build keep the water level high enough so that the entrance to their lodge is never spotted.

Why do some tigers become man-eaters?

Tigers usually avoid humans. Sometimes, though, when they've been injured or become ill, they will go after humans. This is because humans are slower than the animals tigers usually prey on.

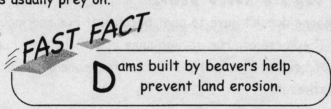

FAST FACT

Dams built by beavers help prevent land erosion.

Hello, I'm Calling the Zoo!

Did you know that animals with double LLs are doubly valuable! As you walk through the zoo, try to spot animals with double LLs. To help you, we've listed a lot of animal words with double LLs in them. How many can you spot?

1. A cousin of the alpaca from South America L L _ _ _
2. Loud cry _ _ L L _ _
3. Canary's color _ _ L L _ _
4. Baby elephant's father _ _ L L
5. Bird's beak _ _ L L
6. Zebra's run _ _ L L _ _
7. What hogs and hippos do in the mud _ _ L L _ _

Solution, see page 131.

Can the porcupine shoot its quills?

The porcupine can't shoot its quills. They are loosely attached and easily removed, though. Any animal taking a swipe at the porcupine or trying to bite it will easily wind up with barbed quills in its mouth or paws.

How can a mongoose outsmart the deadly cobra?

The skilled and brave little mongoose uses its speed and agility to defeat the cobra. It also has a growth of dense, loose hair which protects it from snakebites.

Why can't a horse pant?

A horse doesn't have to pant because it has enormous lungs. The horse can run at high speeds without ever running short of breath. The faster it races, the more air it inhales, or breathes in.

Can the giraffe make sounds? Will it fight?

The giraffe makes a low, throaty sound. Its young, called fawns, bleat like lambs.

The giraffe is a good-natured, intelligent, and affection-ate animal, but it will fight. It uses its long legs to kick. A female giraffe defending her young will take on a lion.

Why do goats eat tin cans?

Goats do not eat tin cans. They will lick off the labels of cans for the glue, which they find delicious, on the backs of the labels.

Giraffes are the tallest animals in the world, with some growing up to 20 feet high.

Horsing Around

There are four different horses, each one ridden by a different person. From the clues given below, can you match the rider with his or her horse? Write the number of the horse in the space provided.

Carla's horse has a mane. Her horse is _____ .
Larry's horse has no mane. His horse is _____ .
Charlie's horse has stirrups. His horse is _____ .
Carrie's horse has stirrups and a mane. Her horse is _____ .

1.

2.

3.

4.

Solution, see page 131.

Why do dogs bark?

Dogs don't have the right kind of voice boxes to speak, so they communicate in other ways. Dogs bark, growl, or whimper. They are trying to tell someone something. It could be a warning, or an alarm, or they're famished, or they're just telling you they're happy to see you.

Dogs also use body language. They will cringe, show their teeth, wag their tails, flatten their ears, and cock their heads. A dog will also raise its hackles—the hair along the neck and spine. They have a very large vocabulary of body language!

Why do dogs chase cats?

Dogs were once hunters. They will chase any small animal. They won't chase cats if they're trained not to.

dog and cat

Are dogs descended from wolves or jackals?

Wolves, jackals, dogs, and foxes may all be descended from the same common ancestor.

Why does a dog always walk round and round before it settles down?

Just like its ancestors and cousins in the wild, it's matting down the grass and making a comfortable spot. So even if it's walking around and around on a place where there is no grass, it's "remembering" an old, old habit.

Why do dogs eat grass?

Besides eating the meat they hunt, the dog's wild cousins, wolves and coyotes, will eat berries and grass. Perhaps the grass tastes good.

Some scientists believe dogs will eat grass when their stomachs are upset. The grass makes the dog throw up whatever it ate that is making it feel sick. Eating grass is also a way for dogs to gather information about their surroundings. They can pick up the scents of other animals that might have been in the area.

FAST FACT

The sense of smell is a dog's sharpest sense.

Pooch Employment Agency

Draw a line to match the dog with the type of work it is known for doing.

Dog Breeds	Type of Work
1. Labrador retriever	a. herding sheep
2. Doberman pinscher	b. service dog
3. Border collie	c. guard dog

Solution, see page 132.

Why do cats like catnip?

There's a chemical in catnip, nepetalactone, that makes cats feel good. Some other cats, including bobcats and cougars, also respond to the aroma and taste of catnip.

Why do cats' eyes glow in the dark?

Cats have a layer of specialized cells in their eyes that reflect and increase incoming light. This makes the cat's eyes glow. It's also why a cat's vision is much sharper than a human's.

Why do cats dislike water?

Not all cats hate water. Certain domestic cats, like Turkish angoras, like it. The big cats that come from hot areas, such as tigers and lions, like it also. The tiger will swim for long distances.

Big cats from cool regions don't seem to like water. Siberian tigers, bobcats, and cougars go out of their way to avoid it, although they will swim if forced to.

One variety of cat is really a water lover. In fact, its feet are partially webbed. The fishing cat of India and Pakistan lives in swamps and along rivers, and even dives for fish.

From what kind of cat is the domestic cat descended?

The direct ancestor of today's house cat was probably an African variety of the European wildcat. The European wildcat is nearly extinct and is protected by law.

What purpose do cats' whiskers serve?

Cats' whiskers, or barbels, are organs of touch. They gives the cat an extra advantage when it's prowling at night.

Catch as Catch Can

Each of these four cats is missing something that is present in the other three. Can you spot all four missing parts.?

1.

2.

3.

4.

Solution, see page 132.

Why does a potato have "eyes?"

Potato eyes are actually buds from which new stems will sprout.

Why do sycamore trees shed their bark?

Most trees have bark that can stretch and expand. However, the sycamore's bark is rigid, and can't expand with the growing trunk and limbs. Therefore, as the tree grows, the old reddish brown bark flakes off, leaving irregular scales where the smooth, greenish white inner bark has been exposed.

Why can't you grow other plants near a walnut tree?

The walnut tree produces chemicals to prevent the growth of other plants near it. This gives the walnut tree more room to grow.

Why are cucumbers, eggplants, and tomatoes called fruits? Aren't they vegetables?

Fruits are fleshy and contain seeds. Vegetables are any plants or parts of plants that are eaten. We call tomatoes vegetables, but they're really fruits, because they're fleshy and contain seeds. Cucumbers, peppers, eggplants, okra, squashes, and melons may be eaten as vegetables, but they are also fruits, because they are the fleshy parts of plants that grow from flowers and contain seeds. Lettuce, carrots, and broccoli have no seeds, and so they are vegetables.

Walnuts are among the oldest food-bearing trees. People eating walnuts date back to about 7,000 BC.

What's This Growing in My Garden?

Can you figure out what plant, tree, flower, shrub, or vegetable these clues are describing?
Here is an example: This four-letter word for a tree starts with an L and ends with an E. Its fruit looks like a green lemon. Answer: lime.

Walnut tree

1. This seven-letter word for a tree starts with an H and ends with a Y. It gave President Andrew Jackson his nickname.

   _ _ _ _ _ _ _

2. This five-letter word for a tree starts with an M and ends with an E. Its sap is poured on pancakes. _ _ _ _ _

3. This five-letter word for a plant starts with a T and ends with an E. It sounds like it should be called the "the hour-plant." _ _ _ _ _

4. This six-letter word for a plant starts with a C and ends with an R. Its four-leafed variety is considered lucky. _ _ _ _ _ _

5. This nine-letter word for a flower starts with an M and ends with an R. Was it the official flower of the Pilgrims? _ _ _ _ _ _ _ _ _

23

Solution, see page 132.

Why is the grass green and a rose red?

The grass is green because it contains chlorophyll, a green pigment that grass uses to change sunlight into food and energy. Roses are red (and violets are blue) to attract bees and other pollinators.

Why do some plants, such as roses, have thorns?

Animals that eat plants will stay away from painful plants with thorns, allowing the plants to survive and produce seeds.

Roses

Why do leaves change color in the fall?

Chlorophyll, which makes leaves green, stops being produced at the end of summer. Then we can see the other colors that were hidden by the green. For instance, the sugar maple's flame-red and orange, the poplar's yellow, and the ash's purple are only seen in autumn.

Why does poison ivy make you itch?

Poison ivy, and its cousins, poison oak and poison sumac, carry an oil, or resin, in their sap that can produce an allergic reaction. Handling the leaves, the berries, or the broken stems can make you itch. Even the smoke of burning poison ivy can be irritating.

How do greenhouse plants produce blossoms out of season?

To produce off-season vegetables and flowers, greenhouses grow plants in liquids without soil. The foods that plants need to grow and flourish are added right to the liquid in measured doses. This method of growing plants without soil is called hydroponics.

FAST FACT

Poison ivy has some likable cousins as well. It's related to the cashew, the mango, and the pistachio.

Guess the Green Word

Fill in the line blanks with the correct words from the list on the right.

1. Green with _____ (jealousy)
2. Green _____ (gardening skills)
3. Green _____ (dollar bill)
4. Green _____ (Special Forces)
5. Green _____ (rookie)

back
beret
envy
horn
thumb

Solution, see page 132.

Why doesn't moss have flowers?

Mosses do not have flowers because they reproduce through spores instead of seeds.

Why is the ginkgo tree called a living fossil?

The ginkgo, or maidenhair tree, is a beautiful tree that can be seen growing on the streets of cities all over the world, as well as in Chinese and Japanese temple gardens. More than 275 million years ago, it was abundant everywhere. However, it no longer grows in the wild. It is a living reminder from the past.

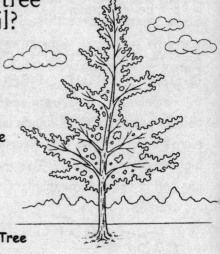

Tree

Why is the mistletoe called a parasite?

Mistletoe is a plant parasite, or a plant that lives on other plants. It never takes root in the ground. Instead, it gets its nutrition and support from the plant it lives on.

Why do plants need light to grow?

Leaf cells in plants use the energy from sunlight to turn water and the gas carbon dioxide into carbohydrates and sugars. This is food plants use.

Why don't all plants die in winter?

While some trees lose their leaves in the fall, they do not die. Instead, they go into a dormant period. They begin growing again in the spring. Many plants, grasses, and shrubs also go into a dormant period during the winter. Some plants reverse this. In the desert, some plants go dormant in the dry summer and grow in the winter, when they can get moisture from rain and snow.

FAST FACT

Other plants that use spores instead of seeds are ferns and liverworts.

Plant Puzzle

Fill in the puzzle with the words from the word list. Use the clues to help you.

1.
2.
3.
4.

Word list
flowers
lime
roses
weed

1. _____ are red
2. April showers bring May _____
3. Lemon and _____
4. Grow like a _____

27

Solution, see page 132.

Why are green plants placed in a freshwater aquarium?

Plants add beauty and realism to an aquarium. They are also needed for the good health of the fish. The green plants remove carbon dioxide from the water and give off oxygen, while the fish use oxygen and exhale carbon dioxide. Fish waste fertilizes the plants, and the fish eat the plants and the little organisms that live around the plants. Plants let the fish hide as well.

fish tank

Why do farmers think that clover is lucky?

Besides being an important hay and pasture plant, clover also enriches the soil. Unlike other plants, clover and other legumes put back into the soil nitrates, which act as fertilizers.

Why do the roots of mangrove trees grow above, instead of below, the soil?

    Mangrove trees are very useful plants that grow in tropical swamps near the coast. There the soil is so wet and dense that underground roots would have to struggle to get enough oxygen, which the tree needs in order to grow. So the mangrove tree has its vine-like roots up in the air! There the roots can absorb the oxygen right through their pores! Because the water in the swamp is so salty, mangrove trees actually filter out the salt from the water.

FAST FACT

The mangrove is useful because it protects coastlines from erosion.

Secret Garden Code

Use the symbols to solve the code and read a favorite saying.

A	B	C	D	E	F	G	H	I	J	K	L	M
@	#	$	%	^	&	*	(	)	+	|	~	<

N	O	P	Q	R	S	T	U	V	W	X	Y	Z
>	¢	£	¥	§	©	®	°	µ	¿	*	_	□

_ ¢ °   @ § ^   ® (^

@ £ £ ~ ^   ¢ & < _ ^ ^

Solution, see page 132.

How can plants live in the desert?

Some plants in the desert have wax on their leaves. This keeps water from escaping. Cacti have thick stems that can hold a lot of water. The stems have a tough skin that thirsty animals can't break. The sharp spines of the cactus also keep animals away.

Why do some desert plants flower so quickly?

Some desert plants patiently wait for the right time to show their true colors. When it rains, the plants quickly come to life. They sprout, show their beautiful flowers and produce seeds, all in a few days.

How can you figure out the age of a tree?

By counting the rings in the stump you can tell the age of the tree. The rings are thick in years of good rainfall and thin in poor years.

Why do some plants eat insects?

Some plants eat insects and other small creatures in order to obtain food that they can't get from the poor soil around them. The pitcher plant and Venus's-flytrap are among the best known of these. They have developed ways to attract their prey. These include sweet nectars and bright colors.

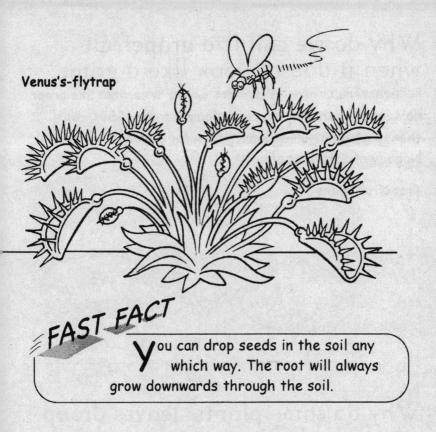

Venus's-flytrap

FAST FACT

You can drop seeds in the soil any which way. The root will always grow downwards through the soil.

Double Plantings

Many words dealing with plants have double meanings. For instance: Which plant word means both a flower and got out of bed? Answer: ROSE Try to identify the words from the clues below.

1. Word for a place where coins are made and an herb?

2. Word for a wise man and an herb?

3. Word for to annoy and a stinging plant?

4. Word for part of the hand and a tree?

Solution, see page 132.

Why do we call it a grapefruit when it doesn't look like a grape?

Grapefruits hang in clusters on the tree, just like grapes do. Grapefruits only became popular in the 1880s. Until then, grapefruit trees were grown for decoration only. Nobody ate the grapefruits!

Grapefruit trees

Why do some plants' leaves droop when touched?

Touching a leaf of a sensitive plant like the touch-me-not changes the water pressure within the leaf. This causes the leaf to move. Other sensitive plants fold their leaves when touched.

Why should people stay away from the New Zealand tree nettle?

The poisons in the stinging hairs on the leaves of the tree nettle are very dangerous. Dogs and horses have died after brushing against the leaves of this 10-foot-high plant.

Why do apples discolor when they are peeled?

Oxygen turns the peeled fruit brown. This happens to pears, peaches, and apricots. Bananas turn brown even when they're not peeled, because their skins are not as strong as apple skins, and oxygen seeps in. Oxidation also makes tea leaves turn a coppery color.

FAST FACT

Certain insect-eating plants trap insects when their leaves or other parts are touched.

Planted Words

Can you find these plant-related words buried in the word grid: APPLE, GRAPEFRUIT, LEAF, SAP, WOOD. Look across and down.

L	E	A	F	A	D	B	D	Z	S
M	J	T	O	P	B	W	O	O	D
R	K	V	G	P	G	G	E	L	O
S	Q	S	H	L	T	U	A	F	P
A	Y	A	T	E	Y	J	F	E	E
B	Z	P	S	W	P	S	Y	D	V
G	R	A	P	E	F	R	U	I	T
K	K	Y	J	V	M	D	B	D	W

Solution, see page 133.

Why do poultry farmers "candle" eggs?

Eggs are inspected for imperfections by holding them up to a light. Years ago, candles were used to provide the light. Nowadays, it's a bright lightbulb, but the word "candle" is still used.

Why is most bubble gum pink?

When bubble gum was invented almost 80 years ago, pink food dye was the only color around. It was added to the gum to make it more appealing. Ever since then, bubble gum has stayed pink.

Why does food make your mouth "water?"

Food on the tongue stimulates the salivary glands, making the mouth "water", or produce more saliva.

What makes butter yellow?

The yellow color of butter comes from carotene, a pigment that converts to vitamin A. Carotene is found in the green plants that cows graze on.

What makes the holes in Swiss cheese?

The holes, or eyes, in Swiss cheese are made by bacteria that give off harmless carbon dioxide gas. This gas forms pockets, or bubbles, in the cheese.

Why do onions make you cry?

The onion's strong oils mix with moisture in the eyes. This forms an acid that irritates the eyes and causes them to tear.

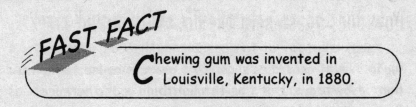
Hidden Eggs

Help the farmer candle the eggs. Some have rolled away and are hidden all over the hen house.

35

Solution, see page 133.

How does yeast help the dough in bread rise?

Yeast is a form of fungus. Its major food source is sugar. Yeast consumes sugar by a process called fermentation. A by-product of this fermentation is the harmless gas carbon dioxide. The gas is trapped in the bread dough and makes the dough expand like a balloon.

If a hamburger doesn't contain any ham, why do we call it a hamburger?

It's named for the city in Germany—Hamburg, Germany—where it was first made.

Why doesn't honey spoil?

Honey has a high acid content, and things that might spoil it, like bacteria, can't survive in it.

Why are certain small fish called sardines?

These small fish were abundant off the coast of the Italian island of Sardinia.

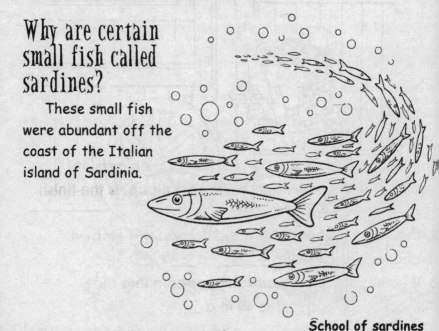

School of sardines

Why is the fig newton named for Sir Isaac Newton?

It's not. It's named for Newton, Massachusetts, a town near where fig newtons were first baked.

What kind of food was sold in the first restaurant?

The first restaurant in the world opened in 1765, in Paris. Nothing but soups were sold. The sign outside offered "restaurants," which means "restoratives or energy boosters." When more of these places opened, they called themselves restaurants, and they added other foods to the menu.

FAST FACT

Because the first restaurants were French, restaurants still use a lot of French terms, like "menu" and "à la carte."

Eating Well

Can you fill in the blanks for these words that end in EAT?

1. In a cooking contest, when the kitchen gets hot and all the contestants tie for first place, is the finish a _ _ _ _ _ E A T?
2. In Holland, when everybody pays for their own chocolate, is that a _ _ _ _ _ _ _ EAT?
3. If you carry a big carton of popcorn into the theater, do you get to sit in a _ _ _ _ EAT?

37

Solution, see page 134.

Why is the sky blue?

Blame it on our atmosphere. Sunlight reaching the Earth makes the sky blue.

The sun's white light is made up of many colors. These colors are red, orange, yellow, green, blue, indigo, and violet. When sunlight comes through our atmosphere, it is scattered by dust particles. The different shades of light are separated. During the day, when the sun is high in the sky, blue light is scattered the most, so we see a blue sky during the day.

Why is the sky clearest in winter?

The sky is clearest in winter, in the morning after a rainfall, from a mountain, or over the ocean. That's because dust particles in the air are smaller at those times and places. The smaller the dust particles, the less the sun rays will be scattered, and therefore the clearer the sky.

Why do we have colorful sunsets?

The sky changes color at sunset because the sun drops on the horizon. Sunlight then has more atmosphere to pass through before it reaches us. Orange and red are able to travel this distance. This is why we see orange and red at sunset.

Sunset

FAST FACT

The core of the sun has a temperature of about 27,000,000° Fahrenheit.

Fun in the Sun

How many words can you make out of the word SUNBATHING? Can you get 10?

_____   _____

_____   _____

_____   _____

_____   _____

_____   _____

Solution, see page 134.

Is daylight the same the world over?

No. Daylight is the period of natural light between dawn and dusk. This can change, depending on where you are and when.

If you're in the polar regions during the summer, you'll experience 24 hours of daylight! We call that the midnight sun.

Just how big is the sun?

The sun is big and old. It is the largest body in the solar system. Its diameter is 865,036 miles. (Earth has a diameter of 7,926 miles.). The sun is five billion years old.

Why does the sun seem small to us?

From Earth the sun looks small, because it is far away. Its average distance from Earth is 93 million miles. Even at that distance, the sun is the nearest star to Earth. Light from the sun takes about eight minutes to reach Earth. This light is still strong enough when it reaches Earth, however, to hurt our eyes if we look straight at the sun.

Eclipse

What's the reason for an eclipse of the sun?

The sun's light is blocked when the moon moves between it and the Earth. The shadow of the moon falls on the Earth. This is a solar eclipse.

How long can an eclipse of the sun last?

The longest a solar eclipse can last is 7 minutes, 31 seconds. The longest total solar eclipse took place on June 20, 1955. It lasted 7 minutes, 8 seconds.

FAST FACT

The surface of the sun covers more than 2,200,000,000,000 square miles.

Sun Fun

Draw yourself taking part in an activity that you enjoy doing on a sunny day.

41

Solution, see page 134.

Which planet goes around the sun the fastest?

The planet that goes around the sun the fastest is Mercury. It orbits the sun at an average speed of 107,000 miles per hour. This is almost twice as fast as the Earth's orbit. Mercury is also the smallest planet, with a diameter at its equator of only 3,031 miles. A year on Mercury lasts just 87.99 days, or about three months.

The solar system

What is the moon?

It is a ball of rock floating in space and held in place by the gravity of our planet. It is the Earth's only natural satellite. As Earth orbits the sun, the moon orbits Earth.

Why does the moon change its shape?

The moon really doesn't change its shape, we just think it does. What we're seeing is an area of the moon lit by sunlight. As the moon circles the Earth, it catches a different part of the light of the sun. These parts, or phases, change as the moon moves around Earth.

Why do we call a period of 30 days a "month?"

The word "month" comes from the word "moon." A period of about 30 days or four weeks is about as long as it takes for the moon to "wax" (grow) and "wane" (shrink) — change from the new moon to the full moon.

How bright is the brightest star?

The brightest star seen from earth is Sirius in the Canis Major constellation. Sirius, or "Dog Star," is 8.64 light-years away from Earth.

FAST FACT

The moon is less than 240,000 miles away from Earth.

Mixed-up Moon

Unscramble the letters to find the phases of the moon.

1. lulf   _____
2. fhla   _____
3. dlo   _____
4. wen   _____

Solution, see page 134.

How many stars are there?

At latest count, there are about 100 billion stars in the Milky Way, which is the galaxy our solar system is in. In the universe, the number of stars is estimated to be 1 followed by 22 zeros.

Why do meteors leave a trail of fire in the sky?

Because they're burning up. Meteors are the visible path of meteoroids—rocks from space. When they hit our atmosphere as shooting stars, they burn up, thanks to friction. It's similar to what happens when metal is scraped along a stone and sparks fly. Very few meteoroids ever make it to Earth's surface, but when they do, they leave an impact! We call them meteorites, and their calling cards are great big craters. The largest crater created by a meteorite is in Quebec, Canada. It is a pit that is 2-1/2 miles in diameter. The largest meteorite ever found weighed more than 60 tons. It was found in Africa in 1920.

Why do comets have tails of fire?

A comet has been called "a large, dirty snowball" in space since it contains ice. The hot sun turns the ice into gas, which, along with dust, forms the comet's tail, which looks like it's on fire as the comet speeds along.

Who was the first man in space?

That was Yuri Gagarin, a Russian cosmonaut. He traveled 18,000 miles into space on April 12, 1961, and orbited once around Earth aboard the spacecraft Vostok I at 17,000 miles per hour for 108 minutes.

Who was the first man on the moon?

On July 20, 1969, American astronaut Neil Armstrong stepped foot on the moon. He was the first human ever to do so.

FAST FACT

One of Jupiter's moons, Europa, is covered by an ice cap that is 60 miles thick.

Moon Maze

Help the astronaut get back to his moon buggy.

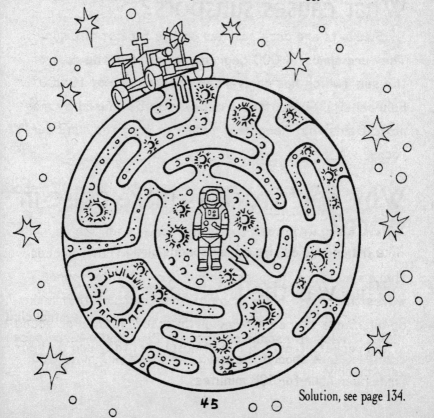

Solution, see page 134.

Why isn't there life on other planets?

The conditions that make life possible on Earth don't seem to exist elsewhere. So far, the temperatures on other planets have been too hot or too cold, and the atmospheres don't support life. This doesn't mean we've stopped looking. It just means that, in our solar system, at least, Earth seems to be the only planet that supports life. Scientists who search for life elsewhere are called exobiologists, xenobiologists, or astrobiologists.

What causes sunspots?

Sunspots are dark patches on the face of the sun. They are almost 4,000 degrees cooler than the rest of the sun, (which has an average temperature of 10,000° Fahrenheit). Sunspots are believed to be caused by magnetic fields that keep heat from reaching the sun's surfaces.

Why don't rockets make noise in space?

Rocket travel is silent in outer space. That's because there's no sound in space. Sound is created by sound waves that cause a vibration of the molecules that make up air. Since there isn't any air in space, there's no sound. When rockets travel in our atmosphere, they can be heard very clearly.

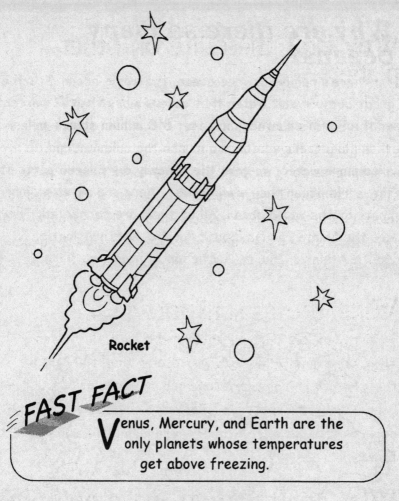

Rocket

FAST FACT

Venus, Mercury, and Earth are the only planets whose temperatures get above freezing.

Planet Puzzler

Match each number to the letter in the code to find which planet names are listed.

A B C D E F G H I J K L M N O P Q R S T U V W X Y Z
1 2 3 4 5 6 7 8 9 10 11 12 13 14 15 16 17 18 19 20 21 22 23 24 25 26

A) 22 5 14 21 19 _____

B) 5 1 18 20 8 _____

C) 13 5 18 3 21 18 25 _____

Solution, see page 135.

Why are there so many oceans?

There's really just one ocean, the world ocean. It's the great body of salt water that covers more than 71 percent of the Earth's surface, or about 140 million square miles.

As explorers ventured out into the unknown and discovered more water, we gave these newly discovered parts of the world ocean their own names. There are seven major parts of the world ocean. All of them are connected. They are the North Pacific, South Pacific, North Atlantic, South Atlantic, Indian, Arctic, and Antarctic.

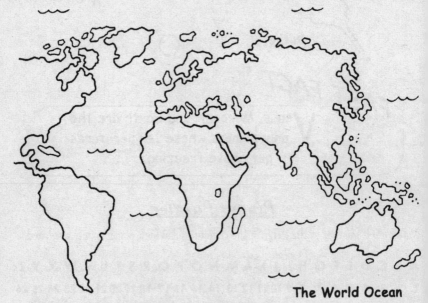

The World Ocean

Why does it rain?

The sun's rays beating down on lakes, rivers, and oceans cause water to evaporate. This water vapor rises up into the atmosphere. It cools and condenses, first into clouds and then into raindrops. The drops fall back to Earth as rain.

Why do volcanoes erupt?

Volcanoes are formed by the build-up of molten rock, or magma, deep inside the earth. This magma forces itself to the surface. It erupts through openings, or volcanic vents, as lava or as hot ash, rock, and dust.

Does the earth quake during an earthquake?

The earth does move, shiver, and shake during an earthquake. It all happens when masses of rock move around rapidly below the Earth's surface. This causes shock waves that open great cracks in the ground and cause landslides and snow avalanches.

FAST FACT

To find out how many miles away a thunderstorm is, count the seconds between the lightning flash and the thunder. Every five seconds is a mile.

Oceanic Confusion

In the sentence below six ocean-related words have been scrambled and turned into other words. Can you spot the ocean words hidden in the sentence?

The heroes in the canoe hurt their hips on the mats. "Eat Kale for what ails you," they were advised.

Solution, see page 135.

How can there be fresh water in the salty ocean?

Two hundred miles out into the salty Atlantic Ocean off the east coast of South America, you can drink fresh water. That's because the Amazon, the largest river in South America, flows into the Atlantic at that point. The mouth of the river is more than 150 miles wide. The Amazon is so huge that 20 percent of all the fresh water on Earth empties into the Atlantic Ocean at almost 32 billion gallons a second. All that water is pushed into the Atlantic so far out that sailors 200 miles at sea can dip a bucket into the salty ocean and still get fresh water!

Why isn't there only one kind of cloud?

Clouds are collections of water droplets or ice crystals or both. Depending on what is in them, they will look different. Clouds are classified as cumulus, cirrus, or stratus clouds. They are further arranged as high, middle, and low clouds, depending on where they are in the sky. Some clouds bring rain or snow, others simply tell us to expect a beautiful day.

FAST FACT

On an average day, the earth has as many as 44,000 storms.

Gone With the Wind

Look at these two pictures of a windy day. They look the same, but EIGHT things are different in the second one. Can you find them all?

Solution, see page 135.

Why is the bottom of the ocean so dark?

Because it's deep. Light can't penetrate the deepest parts of the ocean. Some of the creatures that live so far down carry their own lights with them. Their bodies have light-producing cells. Some creatures of the deep use other senses besides sight to get around.

Ocean

How do we stay on the ground even though the Earth is moving so fast?

Objects are attracted to each other through a force called gravity. The bigger the object, the stronger the pull. Even though the Earth is speeding around the sun at 18.5 miles per second, its large mass keeps us on the ground.

(The Earth weighs 6,595,000,000,000,000,000,000 tons.).
In the same way, the even larger mass of the sun (333,400
times more massive than Earth's) keeps the Earth from flying off into space.

Why does cold weather give us snow?

There are three forms of water: ice, which is the solid
form; water, which is the liquid form; and water vapor,
which is the gaseous form. Water vapor clinging to little
pieces of dust in the air is turned to ice when the temperature falls below freezing. These icy particles become snow
crystals. Crystals that are partly melted cling together to
form snowflakes that fall to the ground.

FAST FACT

The first snow cruiser/motor vehicle for Antarctic
explorers was built in 1939. It was 55 feet, 8
inches long, and almost 20 feet wide. It contained living quarters, a
kitchen, a darkroom, an engine room, and a laboratory.

Which One Does Not Belong?

In each line below, one of the four words does not belong with the others. Circle the
one that does not fit.

1. ocean, lake, teacup, sea

2. sun, moon, planet, broccoli

3. skateboard, ice, snow, hail

Solution, see page 135.

What is acid rain?

When fuels like coal and oil are burned, certain chemicals get into the air. These chemicals dissolve and then fall back to the earth when it rains. These chemicals pollute lakes and streams. They can also damage forests and farmlands. Acid rain can even eat away at the stonework of buildings.

Why does quicksand pull a person in?

When sand gets soaked with enough with water, it's called quicksand. It acts like a liquid. A heavy object can sink in it. A person will find it hard to stand upright in quicksand, but he or she can float on his or her back in it.

Why does a compass point north?

The Earth is a giant magnet. Just like every magnet, the Earth has two poles. These are called the magnetic North Pole and the magnetic South Pole. These magnetic poles are not the same as the geographic North Pole and South Pole. In fact, they are not even close to the geographic poles. The geographic North Pole is called true north. Explorers, sailors, and pilots use maps and navigational charts to find the exact location of true north.

A compass is a freely swinging magnet. Its north-seeking pole is attracted by the Earth's magnetic North Pole and always points in that direction. Everybody who hikes, bikes, camps, or sails should carry a pocket compass. When used the right way, it will keep you from getting lost.

The Chinese used pieces of magnetic rock as compasses back in 2500 BC.

The Needle Points North

These two hikers want to go north. Can you help them get through the maze and headed north?

Solution, see page 136.

Why did people live in caves?

Before there were houses, people sometimes lived in caves for protection against wild beasts and for shelter from the weather. Kentucky has the world's largest cave—Mammoth Cave National Park. In 1798, a hunter chasing a bear rediscovered the opening to the cave, which had once been home to Native Americans. It has 348 miles of charted passageways, which are longer than the entire London subway system and has an underground river.

What causes tidal waves?

An earthquake, an undersea volcano erupting, and even an underwater landslide can cause large tidal waves or tsunamis to wash ashore, often many miles from where the disturbance occurred. In addition to tidal waves, seacoasts are sometimes flooded by storm surges. Storm surges are caused by hurricanes or cyclones and can cause a lot of damage.

What causes a waterfall?

Waterfalls usually develop when a stream or river flows over a cliff and then suddenly plunges downward. A giant waterfall is called a cataract. A smaller waterfall is called a cascade. Waterfalls are used to generate hydroelectric power.

The world's highest-known waterfall is Angel Falls in Venezuela, which drops 3,212 feet down the face of a rugged cliff. It is more than 20 times higher than Niagara Falls. The easiest way to see Angel Falls is from an airplane because it is deep in the jungle.

Angel Falls

FAST FACT

A ngel Falls was named for James C. Angel, an American aviator and explorer, who had discovered the falls after he made a forced landing on a nearby mesa in 1935.

Water Words

How many words can you make from the letters in the word WATERFALL? We found ten.

1. _____
2. _____
3. _____
4. _____
5. _____

6. _____
7. _____
8. _____
9. _____
10. _____

57

Solution, see page 136.

What makes tides rise and fall?

The tides are the regular rise and fall of the ocean and other very large bodies of water, including gulfs and bays. The gravity of the moon pulls the oceans on the side of the Earth facing the moon. This raises the sea level. The highest tide is spring tide. This occurs at the time of a new moon. The lowest tide is called neap tide. This occurs when the moon is in its first or third quarter.

Why is climbing very high mountains so difficult?

Climbers need strength, coordination, and balance. They have to work as a team with other climbers.

Mountain climbing calls for knowledge, experience, and alertness. There are always the dangers of crumbling rock, avalanches, ice, and bad weather, including lightning. There's also the danger of altitude sickness. At high altitudes, there's not enough oxygen in the air and that makes it hard to breathe.

All this work and danger is why mountain climbers who reach the top of very high mountains are praised and honored.

Why do we hear thunder after a flash of lightning?

When electricity builds up in a thunder cloud, and raindrops and hail smash into each other, electricity is discharged. This is a giant spark leaping from the rain cloud to Earth as a lightning bolt or flash. Air in the path of the lightning heats up and suddenly expands, sending out compression waves that become claps of thunder.

FAST FACT

The first people to reach the top of Mt. Everest, the highest peak in the world, were Edmund Hillary and Tenzing Norgay. They reached the summit on May 29, 1953.

Sir Edmund Hillary

Mountain Quiz

In each batch of mountain words below, one does not fit in with the other two for the reason in the clue. Can you find the unwanted word in each group?

1. Two of these are high places:
   a. Mountain
   b. Peak
   c. Valley

2. Two of these are mountain systems
   a. Himalayas
   b. Full-backs
   c. Alps

Solution, see page 137.

Why do ocean waves sometimes get so high?

Wind blowing over the ocean lifts the water and causes waves. The stronger the wind, the higher the waves. That's why in a very bad storm, waves have been known to climb as high as 60 feet. Waves breaking against a shore are called surf.

Why do days get longer in winter?

The planet on which we live, Earth, spins around, or rotates. Earth is also orbiting the sun. Both rotation and orbiting are happening at the same time. Part of the year, in the summer months, the North Pole tilts slightly and slowly toward the sun. The sun shines for a longer period each day. This means longer days in the Northern Hemisphere. Up near the North Pole, the day gets to be really long, with about 24 hours of daylight.

At the South Pole, tilted away from the sun, it gets really cold at this time of the year. In July, 1983, the temperature in Antarctica dropped to 128.6° below zero on the Fahrenheit scale. That is the world's record low temperature. (Yes, in July!)

Later, when the South Pole gets its turn and slowly tilts toward the sun, the Southern Hemisphere gets longer and warmer days. The days in the Northern Hemisphere get shorter, and chillier, as it heads into winter.

Why is ice sometimes black?

It's not really black—ice is clear and colorless. Sometimes a layer of ice on a road will be very thin. It's hard to tell that there's ice at all over the black road. That's when traffic reports start warning drivers about "black ice."

Atlantis was a legendary island continent that was supposed to be in the middle of the Atlantic Ocean, but disappeared in an earthquake. It has never been found.

Drawing Atlantis

Draw your idea of what you think Atlantis looked like.

Solution, see page 137.

Why don't we feel mosquito bites while the mosquito is biting?

The female mosquito's actual bite is so light that the victim doesn't feel it. It's only after the mosquito has done biting that the itching begins. The itching is caused by mosquito saliva, which keeps the victim's blood from clotting long enough for the mosquito to suck it up. It's only the female mosquito that bites. The male lives on nectar and water.

Why do we ground electrical appliances?

By connecting one wire of an electrical appliance to the ground, we make the Earth part of the electric circuit. If the appliance is faulty, the current will flow harmlessly to the Earth, instead of damaging property or giving the user a shock.

Some appliances may not be properly grounded, which is why instruction manuals may warn you to disconnect appliances during a thunder storm, when lightning might find its way into your house's wiring.

Why is helium used in blimps?

Blimps, like other airships or dirigibles, need gas that is lighter than air in order to rise. Helium is seven times lighter than air. Hydrogen was once used, but that proved too dangerous, because hydrogen easily burns. Now helium is the only gas used because it will not burn. Next to hydrogen, it is the lightest known gas.

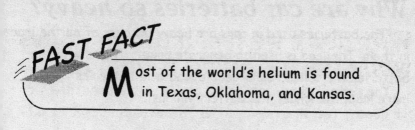

FAST FACT

Most of the world's helium is found in Texas, Oklahoma, and Kansas.

Mixed-up Mosquito

This mosquito got scrambled. Can you put him back in order?

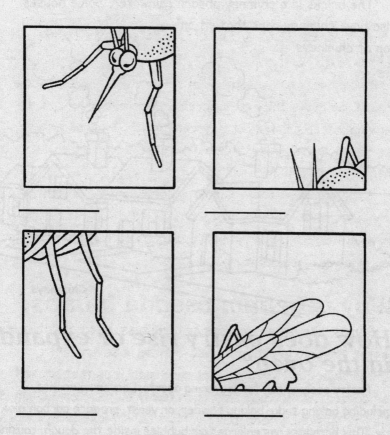

_____

_____

63

Solution, see page 137.

Why are car batteries so heavy?

The batteries used in cars are heavy because of all the lead in them. The lead is used to generate power. This is why the batteries are called rechargeable lead-acid batteries. The more lead, the longer the battery will last.

Why doesn't rain pour down through a chimney in the same way smoke goes up a chimney?

The bricks in a chimney absorb rainwater. Some houses also have chimney caps that sit on top of chimneys.

Chimneys

How does pastry rise or expand in the oven?

Pastry recipes call for leavening agents. Leavening agents, including baking soda, baking powder, or yeast, produce carbon dioxide. This harmless gas enlarges air bubbles inside the dough, causing pastry to rise or expand.

Why is the countryside cooler than the city?

Cities are warmer because of the heat generated by all the people, factories, machines, and cars. Out in the country where things are quieter, it's also cooler!

You'll Need Two Batteries

Can you guess these "battery" words from the clues? Here is an example: This seven-letter word means both a group of cannons and a source of power. Answer: Battery.

1. This four-letter word means both a native of Warsaw, Poland, and either end of a battery.

2. This five-letter word means both to start off and an electric flash when a battery is attached.

3. This four-letter word means both a room in a jail and a battery.

4. This three-letter symbol means both a driver's association and a small battery.

Solution, see page 137.

Why do we hear echoes?

An echo is the reflection of a sound that bounces off an object, such as a mountain, and comes back with enough strength and a little pause in time for it to be different from the original sound. Echoes are important to bats. They make shrill sounds while they fly. The echoes of these shrill sounds help the bats position themselves while they're flying at night. The shrill sounds help bats locate insects as well as buildings.

Why do we see reflections?

When a light wave hits a surface and bounces back to our eyes, we get a reflection. If the surface is very polished flat and smooth, all the light waves bounce off in the same direction. When the surface is a glass mirror with a silvery coating on its back, the light waves go through the glass and bounce off the coating. They then bounce back (reflect) to you, keeping the same pattern that they had before being reflected, except they are reversed. This is why our reflections in the mirror are reversed.

Why do we see shadows?

Light is the reason we see a shadow. When rays from a source of light, whether it's the sun or a flashlight, are blocked by something, we see a dark area within the outline of whatever is blocking the light. We call that dark area a shadow.

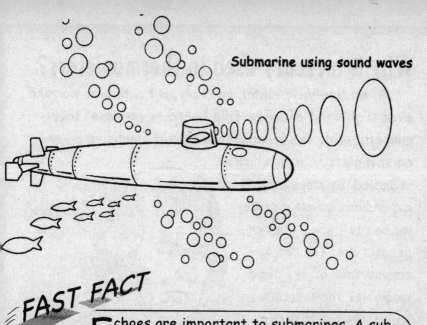

Submarine using sound waves

Echoes are important to submarines. A submarine sends out a sound and when it comes bouncing back, the submarine crew can tell just where they are underwater and who else is around.

Poetry Power

Read the poem below. A word or two is missing from each line. Use the clues to guess the missing word. When you find all the missing words, you will have a complete little poem that was written by Robert Louis Stevenson.

Clues:

1. You, but not you	4. Skull
2. Employ	5. Leap
3. Part of foot	6. Cot

That's Me All Over

I have a little **1** that goes in and out with me,

And what can be the **2** of him is more than I can see.

He is very, very like me from the **3** up to the **4**;

And I see him **5** before me, when I jump into my **6**.

Solution, see page 137.

Why is mercury used in thermometers?

When the liquid metal, mercury, is heated, or warmed even slightly, it expands. In a "mercury-in-glass" thermometer, this expansion means that it climbs up a very narrow glass tube in which it is sealed. By measuring the expansion against a scale, we can tell what the temperature is. The thick curved face of the tube magnifies the mercury so we can see it easily. Gabriel Fahrenheit (1686--1736) invented this type of thermometer in 1714. Fahrenheit also developed the temperature scale that bears his name and is still used in the United States today.

Gabriel Fahrenheit

Why do we call 12 inches a foot?

Because in ancient times, it really was a foot. It was the average length of a grown man's foot. The foot (measurement) was not always the same length. In ancient Greece, the foot was 12.45 inches long. The Roman foot was 11.65 inches long. In early France, the foot was 12.8 inches long. Nowadays, it is always 12 inches long, and one-third of a yard.

Measuring Madness

There are four units of measurement in the sentences below. Each one reads across two words. The first unit of measurement, INCH, is underlined for you. Can you find the other three?

1. "Help me w<u>in! Ch</u>eer me on!" begged the slowest runner in the race. _____

2. "When you arrive in Miami, let me know," his mother said. _____

3. The student took a guess and asked, "Is this figure of speech a noun?" "Certainly," said the teacher. _____

4. "Who is that sitting on top of the hippo?" "Under it, you mean." _____

Solution, see page 137.

Why is a mile called a mile?

It all goes back to Rome. The Roman army estimated five feet to be a pace, or a double step. The mile was based on a thousand paces of the great Roman army as it went on the march. The word "mile" was originally, in Latin, *milia passuum*, or "a thousand paces." A thousand paces equals 5,000 feet. Today's mile is slightly longer, 5,280 feet.

Roman soldier

Why do we abbreviate pound as "lb."?

Our word "pound" comes from the Roman weight *libra pondo*, which means "pound by weight." We remember this in the abbreviation "lb." The British unit of money is a "pound," because it was worth a pound of silver in ancient times. This is still remembered by the symbol for the British pound, £.

Why do countries like France use the metric system to measure things?

France invented the metric system in 1795. The metric system uses meters, liters, and grams, instead of feet, quarts, and pounds, for measuring and weighing. The metric system has been adopted by many other countries. The United States uses it also, especially in science, alongside our standard system of feet, quarts, and pounds.

FAST FACT

The United States passed a law legalizing the use of the metric system on July 28, 1866.

Metric in the Middle

Using a word from the word list, substitute a metric word for the underlined word in each sentence.

1. "Please give me a <u>quart</u> of milk." _____

2. "It weighs six <u>ounces</u>." _____

3. "The town is five <u>miles</u> from here." _____

liter
grams
kilometers

Solution, see page 138.

Why do we count most things by tens?

For numbering most things, we use a system of numbers called a decimal, or base-10, system. The ancient Hindus of India counted things by 10, and their system came down to us.

Why do we divide a year into 12 months, instead of 10?

This idea can be credited to the ancient Romans, who used a base-12, or duodecimal, system of counting. Instead of our decimal system, which uses a base of 10, Romans counted things off by 12. That's why our year has 12 months, our foot has 12 inches, a gross has 12 dozen units, and a dozen has 12 units.

Why is an hour divided into 60 minutes?

Some of our ways of counting things are thousands of years old, going back to ancient Sumer and Babylonia in the Middle East. The Sumerian method of calculating featured divisions based on units of 60, rather than 100. This is called a base-60, or sexagesimal, system. The Sumerians divided the year into 360 days. The hour was divided into 60 minutes, and minutes were divided into 60 seconds. We still use the base-60 system for hours, minutes, seconds, and for measuring circles (360 degrees).

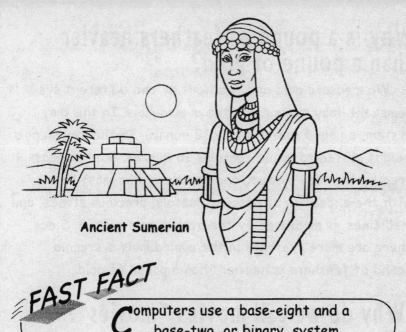

Ancient Sumerian

FAST FACT

Computers use a base-eight and a base-two, or binary, system.

Month Madness

The months of the year are all out of order. Write them in their correct order on the chart.

June	1. _____
April	2. _____
January	3. _____
September	4. _____
May	5. _____
March	6. _____
February	7. _____
August	8. _____
October	9. _____
July	10. _____
December	11. _____
November	12. _____

73

Solution, see page 138.

Why is a pound of feathers heavier than a pound of gold?

We measure gold and feathers by two different systems: the troy system and the avoirdupois. In the troy system, a pound contains only 12 ounces. In the avoirdupois weight system, a pound contains 16 ounces. Gold is measured by the troy system, and feathers, like most things, with the exception of precious metals, precious stones, and medicines, is measured by the avoirdupois system. Since there are more feathers in the avoirdupois system, a pound of feathers is heavier than a pound of gold.

Why do we call movies "movies"?

Movies are made up of thousands of photographs. When a movie is shown, these photographs are "projected" so quickly, one after the other, that they look like they're moving.

Why does a match light?

Special chemicals in matches light, or burst into flame, when they are struck, or rubbed against certain surfaces. There are two kinds of matches: strike-anywhere matches and safety matches. The head of the strike-anywhere match contains all the chemicals needed to burst into flame from frictional (rubbing) heat. Safety matches will only burst into flame when rubbed against a chemically prepared striking surface.

The first movie on film was shown on April 21, 1895. It was a film of a four-minute prize fight.

On the Set

Can you find the 12 differences between these two movie sets?

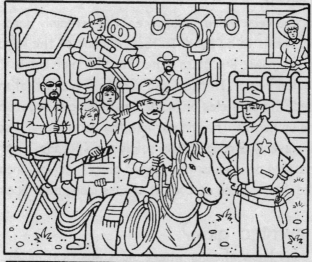

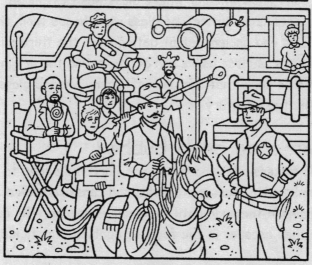

Solution, see page 138.

Why can you see through glass?

You can see through glass because light can pass through it without being scattered or stopped. It's almost as if the glass weren't in the way of the light. This is called transparency.

Why does glass shatter, rather than break in neat pieces?

Glass is a very weird substance. It is certainly hard to the touch. It seems to be solid. In fact, it's one of the hardest substances known. But glass is neither solid nor liquid. It's a "supercooled liquid." In the rapid cooling process that makes glass hard, the particles or molecules holding it together don't line up neatly. They're not like the particles in a solid, which are evenly arranged, like soldiers on parade. That's why glass shatters or breaks into jagged pieces. If you break a true solid, like a piece of coal, it breaks along neat lines.

Who invented glass?

We don't know when or where glass was first made. The first objects made entirely of glass were beads from the Middle East and ancient Egypt dating from the third millennium BC. That's as close as we can get to dating the origins of glass. We do know that Syrian craftsmen invented glassblowing by the first century BC.

Why are soda drinks bubbly?

Soda makers add a harmless gas, carbon dioxide, to the soda drink under pressure. Bottles and cans are sealed, so the gas remains in the soda until the drink is opened. The carbon dioxide then escapes in the form of bubbles that tickle your nose.

Glassblower

FAST FACT

The first soda water was bottled commercially in 1835, in Philadelphia, Pennsylvania.

Broken Glasses

Can you identify these different glasses and give them their right names from the word list?

1. Glass found in a church.
2. Glass that reflects
3. Glass found in a theater
4. Glass that makes things bigger

Word list

stained
looking
magnifying
opera

Solution, see page 138.

How can submarines go under water and then return to the surface?

Submarines submerge by flooding their ballast tanks with seawater and then diving, using wing-shaped hydroplanes, which work like the fins of fish. When the sub wants to return to the surface, the ballast tanks are emptied of water. The sub then becomes buoyant, or floatable, and heads to the surface.

How does an airplane keep flying?

Thanks to its engines and its special wing shape, an airplane can stay up in the air. The engines push the plane ahead. As the plane moves ahead, air rushes over the wings. When air passes over the curved upper surface of a wing, or foil, it travels faster than the air passing under the flat underside. The fast air above the wing has less pressure than the slower air beneath the wing. The greater pressure of the slower air pushes upward, keeping the plane in the air.

Why does a lightbulb burn out?

The incandescent lightbulb produces light by heating threads (filaments) of the metal tungsten to a high temperature (5,000° Fahrenheit). The heated filaments glow and provide light. Under this great heat, the filament sooner or later burns out. Fluorescent lights are more efficient and last longer.

How can laser beams drill holes in diamonds and also play CDs?

Laser beams are narrow beams of light that can do a lot of things. While most light spreads out when it travels, laser beams remain narrow. They can "read" the tiny patterns on CDs and turn them into sound. They can also be focused to deliver enormous concentrated power to drill holes in diamonds. They can travel very far without losing strength.

Flying Double

Two of these six airplanes are an exact match. Can you find the two that are exactly alike?

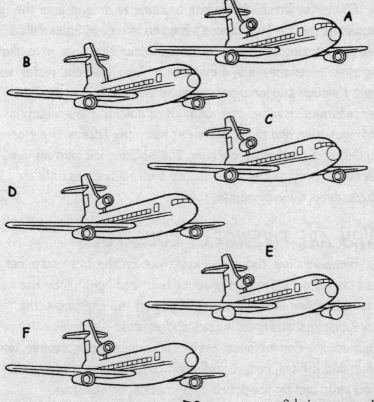

Solution, see page 139.

How do Xrays take a picture of your insides?

Xrays are a form of radiation, like light waves. However, unlike light waves, Xrays can actually penetrate matter.

An Xray photo will show bones and tissues as dark or light areas. Doctors can "read" these photos and make their diagnoses from them. For example, a dentist can look at an X-ray of a tooth and see a cavity deep inside the tooth. A doctor can examine an X-ray of an injured leg and see if the bone is broken.

Why don't skating rinks melt down the way ponds do?

Sooner or later winter has to come to an end, and the ice on a pond melts. That doesn't happen in a rink. Pipes filled with a freezing solution crisscross under the floor of a skating rink. A century ago, a mixture of glycerine and water was sent through copper pipes to make the ice for a rink. This process was slow and the ice melted quickly. Now, electric refrigeration and more efficient methods freeze the floor quickly and for longer periods. Ice hockey, ice skating, ice carnivals, and professional figure skating are possible on these rinks all year round.

Why are fireworks colorful?

Fireworks are two-step explosives. In the first step, certain chemical compounds produce heat and light. Then the heat sets off other chemicals. Depending on the chemicals, the firework displays different colors and effects. Metallic salts produce colors. For instance, barium produces green, copper, and blue; and lithium, red. Sparks and crackles are produced by lead salts and by powdered iron, carbon, or aluminum.

Fireworks

EX-cellent Words

In each batch of four EX- words, one does not fit in with the other three for the reason in the clue. Can you find the unwanted word in each group?

1. Three of these work hard

exert
excavate
exercise
exempt

2. Three of these say something

express
expound
exact
explain

81

Solution, see page 139.

WHY DOES WATER VANISH WHEN IT STARTS BOILING?

It doesn't vanish, it changes to another state. Like all matter, water has three forms: liquid, gas, and solid. Water is a liquid at room temperature. When it boils at 212° Fahrenheit, it changes to a light, thin gas, the gaseous form of water. This gaseous form is steam, or water vapor. When enough of it is boiled off in a small, enclosed space, you can still feel the water, even though you can't see it. We call this sticky feeling dampness, or humidity. On the other hand, if water gets cold enough (32° Fahrenheit), it changes to its solid form, ice.

WHAT MAKES A BOOMERANG RETURN?

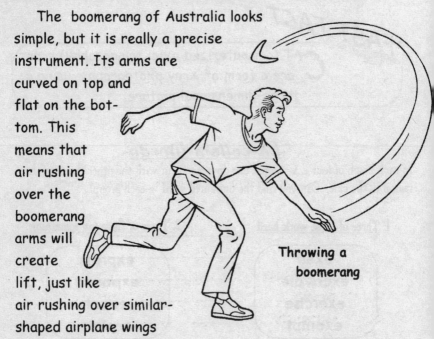

The boomerang of Australia looks simple, but it is really a precise instrument. Its arms are curved on top and flat on the bot-tom. This means that air rushing over the boomerang arms will create lift, just like air rushing over similar-shaped airplane wings

Throwing a boomerang

creates lift. Using an overhand move, it's flipped forward, spinning very quickly. It completes a large circle and then returns to the ground near the thrower.

WHY IS WATER USED TO PRODUCE ELECTRICITY?

The force of falling water is a cheap and efficient way to generate electricity. Water falling over a dam turns turbines that move generators that make electricity. More than 99 percent of electricity in Norway is generated this way. Worldwide, almost 20 percent of electricity is produced through this method, which is known as hydroelectric power (HEP).

FAST FACT

B oomerangs have been used for hunting as well as for fun.

Australian Animals

Unscramble these words letters to find the names of Australian animals.

1. gidon   _____
2. lawbaly   _____
3. agonkroa   _____
4. akalo   _____
5. slapputy   _____

Solution, see page 139.

Why are there so many windmills in the Netherlands?

The Dutch once relied on windmills to produce energy and drain low-lying lands by pumping the water out. Until the invention of steam and electric pumps, the windmill was the major tool for reclaiming the land. By the 19th century, they had built about 9,000 windmills. Many of these windmills are still in use, because the country has few mountains or even high hills to block the wind that operates the mills.

Windmills

What did people wear before earmuffs were invented?

They wore hats and shivered. Earmuffs were invented in 1873 by 15-year-old Chester Greenwood, of Farmington, Maine, where it gets really cold in winter.

Why do we use "Mayday!" as a distress signal?

Originally, in the early 1900s, the international call for help was "CQD." CQD was used by British radio operators and it meant, "All stations attend: Distress." CQD was a poor English way of saying securité or safety in French. CQD was later replaced by "SOS." SOS was easy to pound out on telegraph keys using Morse code, the only way signals could then be sent. That was the radio signal sent from the sinking *Titanic* in 1912, and received by amateur radio operators in the United States. In 1927, the distress signal was changed to "Mayday!," which comes from the French *M'aidez*, meaning "Help me!"

FAST FACT

In addition to pumping water out of low-lying lands, windmills are used to generate electricity.

Which One Does Not Belong?

In each line below, one of the four words does not belong with the others. Circle the one that does not fit.

1. SOS Mayday CQD RSVP

2. earmuffs mittens tennis racket skis

3. windmills dikes canals palm trees

Solution, see page 139.

Why do we have to breathe?

We breathe in order to take in air. Air contains, among other things, oxygen. Oxygen is necessary to change the food we eat into energy so that our bodies can use it to build bone and muscle, and to carry out repair and general maintenance. The lungs remove the oxygen from the air that we breathe and transfers it to very small blood vessels. Oxygen-rich blood is carried to all parts of the body.

Why do babies have more bones than grown-ups?

Babies have 305 bones, but adults have less than 212. That's because some bones fuse together as we grow up.

Why do we snore?

People sleeping sometimes make a hoarse noise. This is snoring. It is caused by the vocal cords and the soft palate in the back of the throat vibrating as the sleeping person breathes. It happens most often when the mouth is open because the nasal passages are blocked.

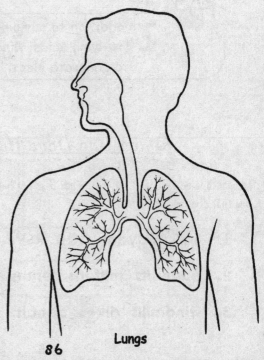

Lungs

Why do we blush?

Sometimes our faces and necks redden when we are embarrassed, ashamed, or confused. This happens when blood vessels close to the surface of the skin expand. That's why we feel warm when we blush. It's involuntary, meaning we have no control over it.

FAST FACT

When we breathe out, or exhale, we send out carbon dioxide and water vapor.

Snorer's Delight

Figure out where to put each of the scrambled letters. They all fit in boxes under their own columns. The letters may or may not go into the boxes in the order they are given. The first column has been completed for you. When you've used a letter, cross it off the top half of the diagram. Do not use it again. Black boxes mark the end of a word. When you fill up the grid, you will find out why a snorer sleeps so well.

N		N		R	R			I	
A	T	L	F	O	S	E	O	H	C	M
S	E	S	H	E	A	N	R	R	E	A
A	■						■		
N		■				■			
S			■						■

Why is our body temperature always 98.6° Fahrenheit?

Humans are warm-blooded. That means our bodies can control our inner body temperature. No matter how cold it is outside, our body's thermostat keeps us at 98.6° Fahrenheit. On the other hand, reptiles and amphibians, such as lizards and snakes, are cold-blooded. Their body temperature changes with the outside temperature. When it's cold outside, their bodies are cold. When it's hot outside, their bodies are hot.

Why do your ears feel "full" in a descending airplane? And why does chewing or swallowing make you feel better?

Have you ever been in an elevator that drops down very quickly? Or in an airplane without a pressurized cabin? Your ears may suddenly get a feeling of fullness. This is because of the sudden change of air pressure. Air pressure pushes in on the ear. This pressure bends the ear drum inward, causing the sense of fullness. When you chew, suck candy, or swallow, this lets the throat muscles open up the eustachian tube, which connects your middle ear with your throat. Air passes upward into the middle ear. Pressure pushes the eardrum back to normal, and you feel better.

Why can't we see in the dark?

When you look at something, what you really see is the light reflecting, or bouncing off the object. This reflected light passes through the eye and falls on the retina, which is a thin membrane lining the back of the eye. The retina takes the light and turns it into impulses, which are sent to the brain as a picture. So without light, there's nothing to see!

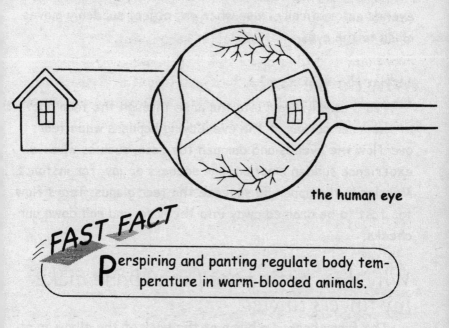

the human eye

Seeing Being

Can you find pairs of rhyming words to fit the clues? Here is an example: Which two rhyming words mean "a creature with sight?" Answer: seeing being.

1. Which two rhyming words mean "a more loyal TV fan?" _____

2. Which two rhyming words mean "a printed glimpse?" _____

3. Which two rhyming words mean "a puzzle stare?"
_____

4. Which two rhyming words mean "a grizzly's scan?"
_____

Solution, see page 139.

Why do we blink?

Tear glands and eyelids act like windshield wipers for the eye. This keeps the eye clean and moist. In addition, the eyelids automatically close when any object suddenly moves close to the eye.

Why do we cry?

Tears usually drain into the nose through the tear duct at the inner corner of the eye. Crying happens when tears overflow the eyelids and dampen the face, such as when we experience sudden emotion, like sadness or joy, for instance. Muscles in the upper lid squeeze the tear glands. Tears flow too fast to be drained away into the nose, and roll down our cheeks.

Why does hitting the funny bone make my fingers tingle?

The funny bone is a bump at the back of the elbow joint. Here, close to the surface, lies a nerve called the ulnar nerve. Striking this nerve will send a sharp pain or a tingling all the way down your arm to your fingers.

Why do we call very smart people geniuses?

In ancient Roman mythology, people believed that a guardian spirit looked over a child. This guardian spirit was called a genius. It was thought that the genius had the power to give success and intellectual powers. This term came to be applied to anyone who was especially gifted, bright, or creative.

Why can I drink something that's really hot without burning myself?

When a hot liquid enters your mouth, a lot of air comes in with it, cooling it. In addition, saliva will help cool it. This doesn't work with very hot liquids, so be extra careful, otherwise you might burn your tongue.

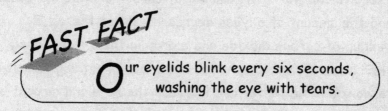

FAST FACT

Our eyelids blink every six seconds, washing the eye with tears.

Hidden Genius

The letters that spell out GENIUS are hidden in this picture. Can you find them all.?

Solution, see page 139.

Why do we breathe faster when we exercise?

There's a part of the brain that controls your breathing rate. It gets signals reporting on how much carbon dioxide and oxygen are in the bloodstream. During active exercise and work, the amount of carbon dioxide increases and the amount of oxygen decreases. When there's a buildup of carbon dioxide and a drop in the oxygen level, the brain tells the diaphragm and other breathing muscles to work a little faster and increase the rate and amount of breathing. Breathing faster gets rid of the extra carbon dioxide and raises the intake of oxygen. When both levels become normal, breathing will slow down.

Why do healing scabs itch?

A scab is a crust of dried blood and fiber that your body produces to protect a wound. As the wound heals, local nerves can get irritated as the scab pulls on the wound. This irritation makes itself felt as itching. When normal skin has been restored, the scab will drop off, and the itching will go away.

Why are some people left-handed?

One out of every 10 people use their left hand for writing. Scientists still don't know the reason for this. Besides a preference for which hand to use, people may have a preferred foot, eye, or ear.

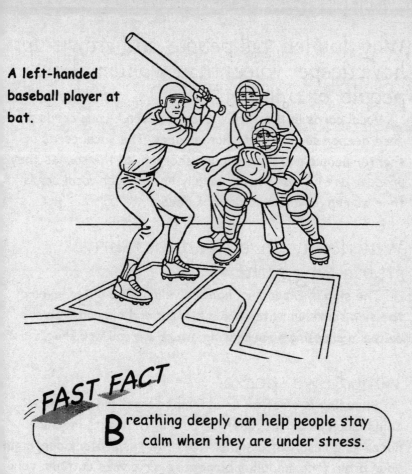

A left-handed baseball player at bat.

FAST FACT

Breathing deeply can help people stay calm when they are under stress.

Get an Earful

How many of these "ear" words can you complete?

1. vanish   __ __ __ __ __ __ **EAR**

2. shoe   __ __ __ __ __ **EAR**

3. tie   __ __ __ __ __ **EAR**

4. British lord   **EAR** _

5. ahead of time   **EAR** __ __

6. merit   **EAR** __

Solution, see page 140.

Why do men, tall people, and grown-ups have deeper voices than women, short people, or children?

Vocal cords in the throat produce sound. Long cords produce deeper sounds than shorter ones. The vocal cords in shorter people and children are shorter, so the sounds they produce are higher. Men generally have longer vocal cords than women, so their voices are deeper.

Why do my fingers and toes shrivel after a long bath?

The skin is expanding, not shriveling. The outer layer of the skin soaks up water like a blotter and expands. This causes a creasing or puckering, which we call wrinkling.

Why do we sneeze?

Sneezing is a reflex or attempt to get rid of something, such as germs, dust, or pollen, that gets in your nose. As a result of a signal from the respiratory center in your brain (the medulla oblongata), air comes up from your lungs. The air quickly moves through your nose to clear it, making the sneezing sound. Other reflexes similar to sneezing are gasping, coughing, and yawning.

Why are some people's eyes blue?

Some people have blue or green eyes, some brown or hazel. It's all in the iris, the part of the eye that controls the amount of light entering your eye. To keep light from being too bright and possibly injuring the eye, the iris is colored with a substance called melanin. The amount of melanin in the iris determines a person's eye color. Less melanin means lighter-colored eyes, while more melanin means darker-colored eyes.

≋ FAST FACT

People with light-colored eyes are more sensitive to the sun.

Why do we have earlobes?

Earlobes are thought to be left over from an early stage of development or evolution. Some believe that earlobes may have been useful in capturing faint sounds. Some people have attached earlobes and others have "free" earlobes. It's just a matter of heredity. Earlobes, like wisdom teeth, the appendix, and tonsils, are called "vestigial," meaning left over or not used any more.

The Ear

Scrambled Words

Can you unscramble these body-related words?

1. ocal crdsvo   _____
2. eesnez   _____
3. inks   _____
4. yees   _____

Solution, see page 140.

Why doesn't food go down your windpipe when you eat?

After food is chewed, it is moved to the throat by voluntary muscles. Then automatic reflexes take over. A flap (called the epiglottis) closes the windpipe. A muscle at the top of the esophagus, or transport tube, opens to let food move into the stomach.

What keeps you from tasting food when you have a cold?

There are smell cells in the nose. These cells are blocked in a nose that's stuffed when you have a cold. The taste cells in your tongue work together with your nose's smell cells, so without the help of your smell cells, they can't do their job and tell you what you are tasting.

Why should you wear a hat in cold weather?

A lot of heat can be lost through the head when you're not wearing a hat. This can be as much as 50 percent of your total body heat.

Hat

Why do your knuckles crack when you pull quickly on your fingers?

When you pull quickly on your fingers, a vacuum is created in the joint space between the bones. This displaces the liquid normally occupying the space. When the liquid rushes back into the empty gap, there's a popping sound.

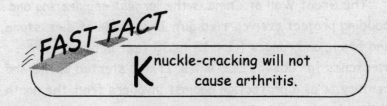

FAST FACT

Knuckle-cracking will not cause arthritis.

Hats Off

From the clues, fill in a style of hat. Then collect all the circled letters to find out what's under all of these things.

1. **Worn by a soldier** Ⓗ __ __ __ __ __
2. **Worn by a Frenchmen** __ __ Ⓞ __ __ T
3. **Worn in the summertime** __ __ __ __ __ W __ Ⓞ __
4. **Worn years ago** Ⓞ __ __ __ __ Y

What's under each of these hats? __ __ __ __

Solution, see page 140.

Why were the tombs of Egypt s pharaohs shaped like pyramids?

It was believed by Egyptians that the spirit of the pharaoh would climb up the steps of the pyramid and join his ancestor, the sun god Ra, at the top. The sides of the pyramid slope down, like the rays of the sun.

Why was the Great Wall of China built?

The Great Wall of China is the largest engineering and building project ever carried out. It is made of dirt, stone, and brick, and ranges from 15 to 30 feet in height. It stretches for about 1,500 miles. It was started in the 3rd century BC as a protection against invaders from the north, and added to in later years.

Why is a book of maps called an atlas?

An atlas is a collection of maps or charts. At one time these collections were decorated with a picture of the Greek mythological figure Atlas holding the earth on his shoulders.

Why does Greenland appear so large on maps?

Maps are not completely accurate. It is hard to depict the curved surface of the Earth on a flat piece of paper. This can result in weird distortions. Greenland, while very large, is sometimes shown to be about the size of South America, which is eight times the size of Greenland.

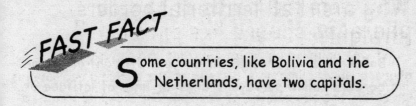

FAST FACT

Some countries, like Bolivia and the Netherlands, have two capitals.

A-Mazing Pyramid

Colorado Bones, the famous Egyptologist, has a problem. He's uncovered the tombs of four Egyptian pharaohs, but in a sandstorm all his notes were blown away. Can you help him make his way through the pyramid to read the mummy's tomb?

Solution, see page 140.

Why aren t all territorial borders straight?

Borders can be straight or curved. Straight or geometric borders follow surveyors' lines, or lines of latitude or longitude. They are usually in places where territory was divided up before people moved in. Many western states, like Colorado or Wyoming, have straight borders for this reason. Curved borders resulted when natural boundaries like mountains or rivers were followed, as in the old countries of Europe.

Why doesn t Louisiana have counties?

Louisiana has 64 parishes, not counties. Louisiana uses the word "parish" instead of "county," as a custom going back to the French and Catholic settlers of the state.

Why is Charleston, South Carolina, called the Earthquake City?

Charleston, not San Francisco, is called the Earthquake City, because of the earthquake of 1886. On August 31 of that year, Charleston was hit by an earthquake that had an estimated Richter scale reading of 6.6. It was the largest earthquake to strike the east coast of the United States, and 60 people were killed.

Louisiana's civil law is based on the French Napoleonic Code, rather than on English common law, but it has been slowly changed to match the system of other states.

Road Trip

Billy lives in Colorado and he's very proud that his state is a rectangle with four straight borders. He wants to drive to Pennsylvania, to visit his cousin Ken, but he only wants to drive through states that have at least two straight borders. Can you draw a line, tracing his trip from state to state?

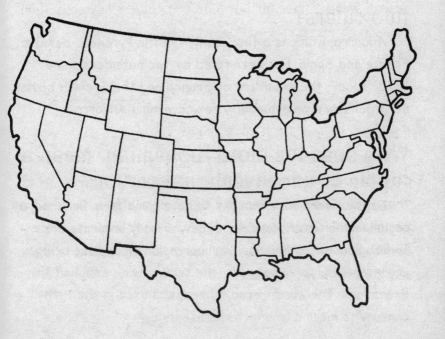

Solution, see page 140.

Why is French spoken in Quebec?

Quebec was founded by the French. Although the British have ruled the region from the 18th century onward, it has always been a center of French culture and language.

Why did Brazil move its capital?

Until 1960, the capital of Brazil was Rio de Janeiro on the coast. A brand-new city called Brasília was then built in the center of the country. Brazil established Brasília as the capital in order to show that it was independent of old colonial ways. Brasília has the widest street in the world, a six-lane boulevard that is 274 yards wide.

Why does the country of Andorra have two rulers?

Andorra, which is a tiny country in the Pyrenees between France and Spain, has been ruled by two outsiders since 1278. Today, the president of France and the Spanish bishop of Urgel share responsibility for governing Andorra.

Why does the word "bohemian" mean a hippie or unconventional person?

Gypsies were once thought to have come from Bohemia, a region in the Czech Republic. (They actually originated in India). Because of the popular impression of Gypsies being unconventional, or vagabonds, the term was also applied to Bohemians. The word, uncapitalized, was used in the 19th century to mean a wild, artistic lifestyle.

Why are there no cars in Venice?

The Italian city of Venice is built on water. Venetians either walk or take a boat to get somewhere. The city is nicknamed "the Bride of the Sea."

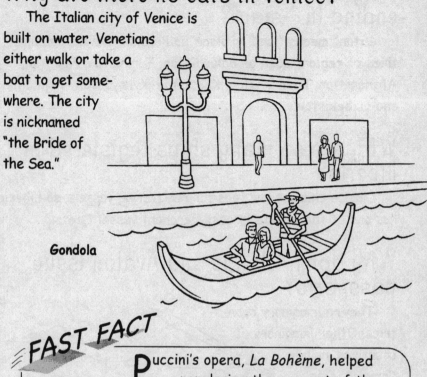

Gondola

FAST FACT

Puccini's opera, *La Bohème*, helped popularize the concept of the bohemian life as being wild and unconventional.

Canadian Sunrise

What do you know about our neighbors to the north? How many of these Canadian trivia questions can you answer?

1. Montreal is in a) Ottawa, b) Alberta, c) Quebec
2. RCMP is a) a Mountie b) an animal rights group
   c) Canadian rock group
3. Vancouver is a) on the west coast b) on the east
   coast c) in central Canada
4. The flag of Canada shows a) stars b) a maple leaf c) stripes

Solution, see page 141.

Why do so many countries have names ending in "-stan"?

"Stan" means "land or place" in Persian. We have countries or regions such as Baluchistan, Turkestan, Pakistan, Afghanistan, Kazarkhstan, Khuzistan, Kyrgyzstan, Tajikistan, and Uzbekistan.

Why are so many ships registered in Liberia?

Liberia charges low fees for registering vessels, so Liberia has one of the world's largest merchant vessel fleets.

Why don't Atlantis and Avalon issue passports?

They're imaginary countries. Other imaginary countries include Camelot (King Arthur's kingdom), El Dorado (a golden kingdom in South America), Emerald City (the capital of Oz), and Middle Earth (in *The Lord of the Rings*).

King Arthur

Why was the former ruler of Russia called a czar?

"Czar" is the Russian version of the name Caesar. Emperor Caesar of Rome represented all that was powerful in a ruler, so rulers after him used his name. The German equivalent is "kaiser."

Why does Switzerland have so many languages?

Switzerland has people of several cultures. There are speakers of German, French, Italian, and a special dialect called Romansch. Despite their language differences, they all get along, and most people in Switzerland speak at least two languages, some even more!

FAST FACT

Panama, like Liberia, also registers a great many merchant ships.

Do you Under-stan?

The word "Stan" means "country." We've taken some well-known countries and changed their names to stan countries. For instance, Peru might be called Andestan. Can you identify the countries we've disguised?

1. **Paristan** _____
2. **Beatlestan** _____
3. **Koalastan** _____
4. **Borschistan** _____
5. **Pastastan** _____
6. **Shamrockstan** _____

Solution, see page 141.

Why don't Icelandic homeowners have high fuel bills?

Many homes in Iceland are heated by hot springs and geysers, instead of by coal, wood, oil, or gas.

Why have African governments created huge national parks?

To protect their wildlife, several countries in Africa have set aside land for the exclusive use of wild animals. These national parks are sometimes thousands of square miles in size. Some have tourist facilities that let visitors watch the animals in a natural setting. Among the countries that have established such parks are Burkina Faso, Cameroon, Kenya, Tanzania, Zimbabwe, and South Africa.

Why is the official home of the president of the United States called the White House?

During its construction, from 1792 to 1800, the gray sandstone walls of the building were painted white. People began calling the building the "white house" because of that. However, the building was also known as the President's House or the Executive Mansion. The White House became the official name of the president's home in 1901.

Why was William of Orange called "The Silent"?

William of Orange (1533-1584) gave his fortune and his life to the cause of Dutch independence and religious freedom. As a young nobleman trained in diplomacy, he heard many state secrets, but revealed none of them, for which he was given the nickname "The Silent."

Why did a petroleum-rich country remain poor for years after the discovery of oil?

Oil was discovered in Saudi Arabia before the Second World War (1939-1945), but work on oil wells halted during the war. The country was left in poverty until after the war ended.

FAST FACT

The White House has been home to every president of the United States except for George Washington (1732-1799). Construction on the White House was not finished until after his presidency was over.

White House Tour

Take a tour of the White House by making your way through this maze.

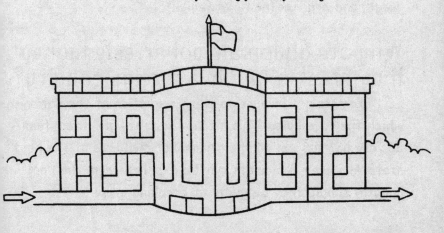

107

Solution, see page 141.

Why do people of Indian descent make up more than half of the inhabitants of the Pacific island of Fiji?

Late in the 19th century, the British brought in Indian laborers to work on the Fijian sugar plantations. Today more than half of all Fijians are of Indian descent.

Why is Northern Ireland sometimes called Ulster?

Northern Ireland is sometimes called Ulster because it includes six of the nine counties that made up the early Celtic kingdom, or province, of Ulster.

Why does Norway have two official dialects?

The Norwegian language belongs to the Scandinavian group and is similar to Danish and Swedish. There are many dialects. There are two official forms—*bokmal* (book language) and *nynorsk* (new Norwegian).

Why are diplomats not arrested when they break a law in a foreign country?

Diplomats are immune to the jurisdiction of the nation in which they are living. This means that they and their families are not subject to the criminal or civil laws of the host state. However, diplomats may be expelled from the host country should they be guilty of breaking a law.

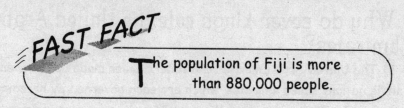

The population of Fiji is more than 880,000 people.

Embassy Row

The ambassador from Middle Slobbovia is new to his post. He's just arrived and he's looking for his embassy. All he knows is that his embassy is different from all the others on Embassy Row, even though they look mostly alike. Can you help the ambassador find his embassy?

Solution, see page 141.

Why do seven kings rule the United Arab Emirates?

The United Arab Emirates is a federal union made up of seven little nations called emirates, which are each governed by hereditary rulers. This means that the power to govern is passed down from family member to family member. The highest federal authority lies with the Supreme Council of Rulers, which consists of the rulers of the seven emirates.

Why did a whole city go on strike?

In 494 BC, the plebeians, or commoners, of ancient Rome went on a general strike. In a body, they marched out of Rome to make a new city. This strike terrified the ruling patricians who agreed to make social changes. For the first time, plebeians were able to elect two representatives, or leaders.

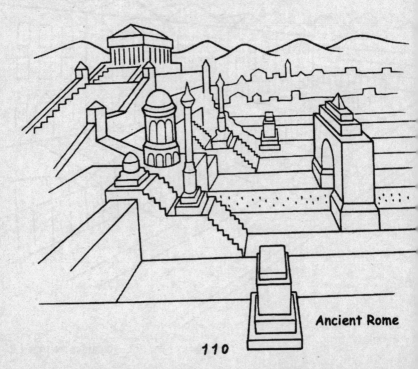

Ancient Rome

Why does the Netherlands need dikes?

Most of the Netherlands' land was once under water. Beginning in the 13th century, dikes were built to take back the land from the sea. A dike is made of earth, built to control or hold back water. By the end of the 20th century, about 2,600 square miles were reclaimed.

FAST FACT

Another form of a dike is called a levee. While dikes protect land that might be under water most of the time, levees protect dry land that may be flooded because of rising water from a river.

MISSING MIDDLE EAST

Part of the name of each of these countries has vanished. Can you find the missing section of each country's name in the word box?

1. IS__ __ __ L
2. LE__ __ __ ON
3. CYP__ __ __
4. S__ __ __ A
5. JOR__ __ __
6. __ __ __ KEY
7. __ __ __ N
8. SAU__ __ __ RABIA
9. __ __ __ Q
10. UNITED ARAB
    EMI__ __ __ ES
11. KU__ __ __ T
12. O __ __ __
13. YE__ __ __

Word Box

RAT
TUR
IRA
MAN
RAE
RUS
MEN
BAN
DAN
DI A
WAI
YRI
IRA

Solution, see page 142.

Why did Botswana name its currency the pula?

"Pula" means "rain," which is highly valued in this land-locked country, where parts of the country are so dry there are no permanent streams.

What makes the Korean alphabet unique?

It is an artificial system of writing, commissioned by the Korean king, Sejong, in 1443. It replaced an earlier system based on Chinese characters. The Chinese alphabet was very hard to learn. Sejong wanted something simple yet logical. He actually helped create the Korean alphabet, called Hangul.

Why was a period in English history called the War of the Roses?

A series of civil wars in England between the years of 1455 to 1485 are called the War of the Roses. The quarrel was between the royal houses of York and Lancaster over the right to rule England. The emblem of the Yorkists was a white rose and that of the Lancastrians a red rose.

Why is the Vatican s Swiss Guard considered the world s oldest army?

The Vatican is protected by the Swiss Guard. The Swiss Guard of Vatican City has its origins in the 1500s. All members come from Switzerland. There are six officers and 110 enlisted men.

Members of the Swiss Guard still wear the traditional uniforms and helmets designed by the artist Michelangelo. Michelangelo is the famous painter of the ceiling of the Sistine Chapel.

Swiss Guard Twins

Two of these six Swiss Guards are exactly alike. Can you find them?

113

Solution, see page 142.

How did the Argentinean region of Mesopotamia get its name?

Mesopotamia, which means "between the rivers," lies between the Paraná and Uruguay rivers. It was named for the ancient region of Mesopotamia in the Middle East. Argentina's Mesopotamia is a humid and fertile lowland.

Why does Belgium have three official languages?

Belgium has fewer than 10 million people, but they are divided along language lines. Dutch is the official language in the north of Belgium, French in the south, and German along the eastern border. Belgium is a nation of Germanic, Dutch-speaking Flemings and Celtic, French-speaking Walloons. In addition, some Belgians are German-speaking.

The Flag of Belgium

Why are the ylang-ylang and coelacanth important to the Comoros?

The Comoros, an African island republic located in the Indian Ocean near Mozambique, grows the ylang-ylang tree because it is a source of perfume. The seas off the Comoros are the home of the famous "fossil" of the coelacanth, which was a fish that was thought to be extinct for millions of years until 1938, when a living coelacanth was caught off the coast of South Africa. From 1952, other coelacanths have been caught off the Comoros.

FAST FACT

Mesopotamia in the Middle East is today's Iraq.

Mesopotamia Words

How many words can you make out of the word MESOPOTAMIA? We found 27 words. If you need to, use an extra piece of paper.

Solution, see page 142.

Why did the 19th-century father of the computer never finish his work?

Charles Babbage (1792–1871) is the English mathematician credited with inventing the computer. However, he never completed his work. Babbage came up with two inventions, the difference engine and the analytical engine. The analytical engine was a programmable device, the forerunner of the computer, long before anyone had ever heard of a mouse, a modem, or a computer virus. But his ideas were too advanced for the technology of the time. So the world had to wait more than 100 years for a computer that matched Mr. Babbage's pioneering ideas.

Why was the first steamboat called "Fulton's Folly?"

Before Robert Fulton (1765–1815) proved it could be done, nobody believed that steam could drive a boat. At the time, boats used only sails. Fulton developed a steamboat in spite of people laughing at him. On August 7, 1807, Fulton's *Clermont* traveled up New York's Hudson River. The 150-mile trip took 32 hours, and the boat traveled under its own steam.

Why did King Alfred let the cookies burn?

The story is told that King Alfred the Great (848–899), one of the best-known names in English history, was fleeing from his enemies. He took refuge in the small cottage of a poor swineherd. The swineherd's wife was baking some cookies, and she told the king (who was in disguise) to watch them and keep them from burning while she did her errands. King Alfred was busy drawing up plans to defeat his enemies and forgot to watch the cookies. When the swineherd's wife returned, the cookies had burned. She yelled at the king, who humbly apologized.

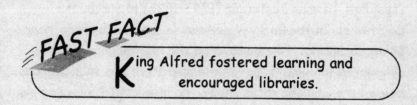

Draw Your Own Steamboat

Imagine you are an inventor in the early 1800s. Draw your own version of a steamboat.

         Solution, see page 142.

Why did Zebulon Pike never climb Pike's Peak?

Captain Zebulon Montgomery Pike (1779-1806) discovered the mountain that's named after him in November, 1806. Captain Pike was heading a band of explorers commissioned by President Thomas Jefferson (1743-1826) to survey the Southwest. In the Rocky Mountains in central Colorado, near Colorado Springs, Pike discovered the high mountain. He attempted to climb it, but the temperature was four degrees below zero, and the rocks showed no interesting animal or plant life, so he and his group turned back. The 14,140-foot mountain was climbed 14 years later by another group.

Why were Roosevelt's Rough Riders considered rough?

Long before he was president, Theodore Roosevelt (1858-1919) organized the First Volunteer Cavalry, just after the outbreak of the Spanish-American War in April, 1898. Commanded by Colonel Leonard Wood, it was a volunteer cavalry regiment brought together to fight the Spanish, who then held Cuba. Instead of regular soldiers, the regiment was made up of a strange mixture of cowboys, sheriffs, businessmen, and polo players. The newspapers dubbed them the

Teddy Roosevelt

Rough Riders. They fought well, and their charge up San Juan Hill entered the history books.

Why was the purchase of Alaska called Seward's Folly?

In 1867, when Russia agreed to sell Alaska, or "Russian America," as it was then called, for only $7.2 million, Secretary of State William Henry Seward (1801-1872) jumped at the chance. Buying 600,00 square miles of wild and frozen land was not popular. His purchase was called Seward's iceberg, Seward's icebox, and Walrussia. Seward coolly ignored the outcry.

FAST FACT

William Seward named the new territory purchased from the Russians Alaska, which is a version of the Aleutian word "Alayeksa," meaning "a great country."

Historic Words

Unscramble these letters to get history-related words.

1. laskaa _____
2. alvaryc _____
3. kepis akpe _____
4. ughro idrers _____
5. ardsews floly _____

Solution, see page 143.

Why was the first electric battery called "Volta's pile"?

It was named for the inventor, Alessandro Volta (1745-1827). In 1800, he piled a number of metal plates together and put them into an acid solution, where they generated electricity.

Why are "comp" tickets called Annie Oakleys?

Annie Oakley (1860-1926) was a star sharpshooter with Buffalo Bill's Wild West Show. She once broke 942 glass balls thrown into the air with only 1,000 shots. Her favorite was the playing card trick. She would throw the five of hearts into the air and before it landed punched holes through all five hearts. Complimentary tickets, free press passes, and free railroad passes were punched with holes, so they were named Annie Oakleys in honor of her terrific sharp shooting.

Why were six towns named after P. T. Barnum?

P.T. Barnum may have been the greatest showman who ever lived. He ran circuses, side shows, and even concerts. He used publicity and advertising to raise interest in his shows, which

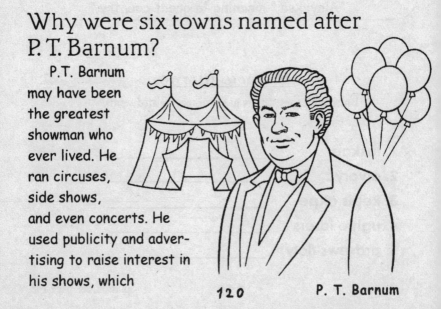

P. T. Barnum

included everything from the original Siamese twins and Jumbo the elephant to the 31-inch-high General Tom Thumb. So popular were his shows that towns named themselves after him.

Why were policemen named after Sir Robert Peel?

Sir Robert Peel was the English politician who reorganized the London police department into an effective force in the 1820s. London police were thereafter called "Peelers" and "bobbies."

FAST FACT

P.T. Barnum served several terms as a Connecticut state legislator and one term as the mayor of Bridgeport, Connecticut.

What's in a Name?

Lots of people have given their names to inventions. Can you match the description to the invention?

1. **Ampere was named for Andre Marie Ampere** __

2. **The Beaufort Scale was named for Sir Francis Beaufort** __

3. **The Bessemer Process was named for Henry Bessemer** __

4. **Chisholm Trail was named for Jesse Chisholm** __

5. **Comstock Lode was named for Henry Comstock** __

<u>Invention</u>

a) **steel making**

b) **electric unit**

c) **pioneer route**

d) **wind-velocity measure**

e) **gold mine**

Solution, see page 143.

Why was a knife named after Jim Bowie?

Colonel James Bowie (1799–1836) was one of the heroes of the Alamo, fighting and dying at the side of his friend Davy Crockett. He was credited with inventing a 15-inch hunting knife that was razor sharp and curved to a point. Bowie killed a man with it in a duel.

Why was Colonel William Frederick Cody called "Buffalo Bill?"

Bill Cody was one of the West's top buffalo hunters at a time when that animal was used as a cheap source of meat and hides. Cody killed 4,280 of them in a single year. Sixty million buffalo roamed the West until the 19th century. The number seemed endless but the buffalo was nearly wiped out, with only 1,000 or so remaining. Early conservationists saved the buffalo. Now there are almost 200,000 of them, and they live as a protected species. Buffalo Bill also invented the Wild West Show and the professional rodeo.

FAST FACT

Buffalo Bill was also a scout and a cavalryman for the U.S. Army.

Hidden Buffalo

There are 12 buffalo hiding from Buffalo Bill Cody. Can you find them all?

Solution, see page 143.

Why did Dr. Seuss win an Oscar?

Besides writing *The Cat in the Hat* and other books for children, Dr. Seuss, born Theodor Seuss Geisel (1904–1991), created the animated cartoon character *Gerald McBoing Boing*, for which he won an Academy Award in 1951.

Why did the author of *Heidi* begin writing?

Johanna Spyri first turned to writing children's stories in order to raise money for the Red Cross. Her books became favorites of children all over the world. She wrote stories about the people and scenes of her childhood in the beautiful Swiss Alps.

What children's book was partly written as a plea for treating animals kindly?

The English author Anna Sewell wrote *Black Beauty* in 1877. It was the first realistic novel about animals and it describes the harsh treatment a horse receives from its masters. Thousands of copies were given away to animal handlers to convince them to treat animals better.

Why did Laura Ingalls Wilder write about pioneer life?

Laura Ingalls Wilder (1867–1957) travelled with her family across the unsettled plains and prairies of the U.S. When she was in her sixties, her daughter suggested that she write about growing up on the frontier during the 1870s and 1880s. That is how *The Little House on the Prairie* was born. It became the first in her beloved series.

FAST FACT

Dr. Seuss's books have been translated into more than 15 languages. More than 200 million copies of his books have been sold around the world.

Laura Ingalls Wilder

State the Book

Rearrange each line of letters to form the name of a state. Then put the letters in the boxes on the line below to spell what Laura Ingalls Wilder lived in.

1. WELEDARA __ __ ☐ __ __ __ __ __

2. SALENPYNANVI __ __ __ __ __ __ __ __ __ __ ☐ ☐

3. NCOTEUCNCIT __ __ __ __ __ ☐ __ __ __ __ ☐

4. DRAMNALY __ __ __ __ __ ☐ __ __

5. WEN SHRIMPHAE __ ☐ __ ☐ __ __ __ __ __ __

6. THOUS RAINCOLA __ ☐ ☐ __ __ __ __ __ __ __ __ __

7. ESNETSENE __ __ __ __ __ __ ☐ ☐ __

__ __ __ __ __ __ __ __ __ __ __

Solution, see page 144.

Why was a brand of artificial grass named Astroturf?

The artificial turf got its name from the Houston Astrodome, where it was first installed in 1965.

Why is a hitless batter called an "ohfer."

If a batter goes hitless four times at bat, he's 0 for 4.

Why was Baby Ruth candy named after the baseball player?

It wasn't. The Baby Ruth candy bar was named for the baby daughter of President Grover Cleveland. Babe Ruth was such a household name, though, that his name was always associated with the candy.

Why is a basketball backboard also called the bankboard?

Players use the backboard to "bank" their shots toward the basket, which means to take shots from an angle, especially lay-ups.

FAST FACT

Babe Ruth's real name was George Herman Ruth.

Spot the Real Basketball Player

Can you spot the real basketball player among these imposters?

Solution, see page 144.

Why are the minor leagues called the "bush leagues?"

Minor league games were once played on sandlots where the bush and undergrowth hadn't been cleared.

Why is a football field called a gridiron?

Its horizontal lines, which are spaced five yards apart, give it the appearance of a griddle.

Why are some college players called red shirts?

These players have been withheld from competition for a year in order to extend their eligibility to play. In NCAA sports, athletes have four years of being eligible to play sports and five years to use that eligibility. So if an athlete is not ready physically or academically, he or she is allowed to spend their freshman year practicing with their team but not playing in any official games. The term, red shirts, comes from the red jersey worn by these young players.

FAST FACT

The word "scrimmage" comes from the word "skirmish," meaning "a little battle."

Quarterback

Sports IQ

Can you identify these sports words from the clues?

1. This four-letter word begins with a G and ends with an F, and is played on a fairway. _____

2. This five-letter word begins with a V and ends with a T and is a move in gymnastics. _____

3. This six-letter word begins with an S and ends with an M and is skiing in a zigzag way. _____

4. This eight-letter word is another term for table tennis. _____

Solution, see page 144.

Solutions

Page 3

```
D   I   N   O   S   A   U   R   X   P
F   D   F   E   R   E   Z   X   T   T
R   Q   W   E   R   Q   E   V   R   E
E   W   E   R   G   H   J   K   N   R
P   O   Z   M   P   Q   J   E   C   O
T   A   G   S   J   D   K   C   M   S
I   O   E   F   O   S   S   I   L   A
L   X   V   T   Y   K   L   A   S   U
E   K   L   J   E   G   R   A   E   R
D   G   E   F   S   P   O   R   H   S
```

p. 5

p. 7
TURTLE, SNAKE, ALLIGATOR, GECKO, LIZARD, RATTLER

p. 9
1. bald eagle
2. hoot owl
3. fly-catching warbler
4. meadow lark
5. yellow-bellied sapsucker

p. 11
BEE BET BAT OAT OFT AFT ANT
BUG BAG SAG SAY SLY FLY

p. 13
1. SALMON; 2. MINNOW; 3. SHARK; 4. SARDINE; 5. CARP

p. 15
1. Llama, 2. Bellow, 3. Yellow, 4. Bull, 5. Bill,
6. Gallop, 7. Wallow

p. 17

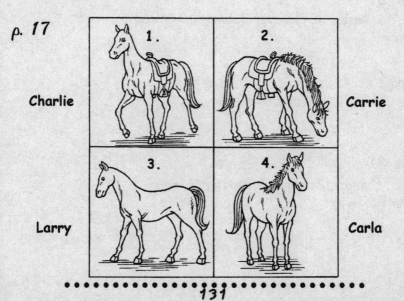

Charlie — 1.
Carrie — 2.
Larry — 3.
Carla — 4.

••••••••••••••••••••••••••••••••

p. 19
1. B   2. C   3. A

p. 21
1. tail;   2. yarn;   3. whiskers;   4. mouse

p. 23
1. Hickory;   2. Maple;   3. Thyme;   4. Clover;   5. Mayflower

p. 25
1. Green with envy;   2. Green thumb;   3. Greenback;
4. Green Beret;   5. Green horn

p. 27
1. Roses;   2. Flowers;   3. Lime;   3. Weed

p. 29
You are the apple of my eye.

p. 31
1. mint;   2. sage;   3. nettle;   4. palm

p. 33

L	E	A	F	A	D	B	D	Z	S
M	J	T	O	P	B	W	O	O	D
R	K	V	G	P	G	G	E	L	O
S	Q	S	H	L	T	U	A	F	P
A	Y	A	T	E	Y	J	F	E	E
B	Z	P	S	W	P	S	Y	D	V
G	R	A	P	E	F	R	U	I	T
K	K	Y	J	V	M	D	B	D	W

p. 35

· ·

p. 37
1. Dead heat
2. Dutch treat
3. Box seat

p. 39
BAG BAN BANG GIN GUN HANG HUN HUNG NUT
SHIN SHUN SING STING STUN STUNG SUN SUNG
TAG TAN TANG THING THUG TIN

p. 41
Answers will vary.

p. 43
1.full; 2. half; 3. old; 4. new

p. 45

•••••••••••••••••••••••••••••••••

p. 47

   A. Venus; B. Earth; C. Mercury

p. 49

   canoe = ocean; hips = ship; mats = mast;
   kale = lake; ails = sail

p. 51

p. 53

   1. teacup; 2. broccoli; 3. skateboard

p. 55

p. 57

1. all
2. ate
3. eat
4. fall
5. fat
6. real
7. tell
8. wall
9. water
10. well

p. 59
1. c 2. b

p. 61
Answers will vary

p. 63

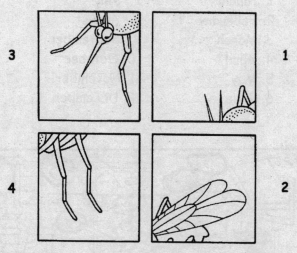

p. 65
1. pole; 2. spark; 3. cell; 4. AAA

p. 67
I have a little 1) shadow that goes in and out with me,
And what can be the 2) use of him is more than I can see.
He is very, very like me from the 3) heels up to the 4) head;
And I see him 5) jump before me, when I jump into my 6) bed.

p. 69
1. INCH
2. MILE
3. OUNCE
4. POUND

p. 71
1. Liter
2. Grams
3. Kilometers

p. 73
1. January
2. February
3. March
4. April
5. May
6. June
7. July
8. August
9. September
10. October
11. November
12. December

p. 75

p. 77
1. stained glass; 2. looking glass; 3. opera glass;
4. magnifying glass

p. 79
A and C

p. 81
1. exempt
2. exact

p. 83
1. dingo; 2. wallaby; 3. kangaroo; 4. koala; 5. platypus

p. 85
1. RSVP
2. tennis racket
3. palm trees

p. 87

A		S	N	O	R	E	R		C	A
N	T		H	E	A	R		H	I	M
S	E	L	F		S	N	O	R	E	

p. 89
1. truer viewer; 2. book look; 3. maze glaze;
4. bear glare

p. 91

139

p. 93

    1. disappear; 2. footwear; 3. neckwear; 4. earl; 5. early; 6. earn

p. 95

    1. vocal cords

    2. sneeze

    3. skin

    4. eyes

p. 97

    1. Helmet; 2. Beret; 3. Straw hat; 4. Derby HEAD

p. 99

p. 101

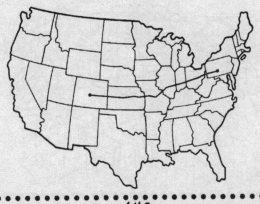

....

p. 103

1. c; 2. a; 3. a; 4. b

p. 105

1. France
2. England
3. Australia

4. Russia
5. Italy
6. Ireland

p. 107

p. 109

p. 111

1. Israel	8. Saudi Arabia
2. Lebanon	9. Iraq
3. Cyprus	10. United Arab
4. Syria	Emirates
5. Jordan	11. Kuwait
6. Turkey	12. Oman
7. Iran	13. Yemen

p. 113

A and C.

p. 115

1.	AIM	15.	POT
2.	AIMS	16.	POTS
3.	MATE	17.	SOOT
4.	ME	18.	SOP
5.	MESA	19.	SPAM
6.	MET	20.	SPIT
7.	MIME	21.	SPOT
8.	MIMES	22.	TAME
9.	MOOSE	23.	TAMES
10.	MOP	24.	TAMP
11.	MOPS	25.	STAMP
12.	PITS	26.	TIME
13.	POEM	27.	TIMES
14.	POEMS		

p. 117

Answers will vary.

p. *119*

1. Alaska
2. Cavalry
3. Pike's Peak
4. Rough Riders
5. Seward's Folly

p. *121*

1. b; 2. d; 3. a; 4. c; 5. e

p. *123*

p. 125

1. Delaware
2. Pennsylvania
3. Connecticut
4. Maryland
5. New Hampshire
6. South Carolina
7. Tennessee

Little House

p. 127

The real basketball player is C.

p. 129

1. golf; 2. vault; 3. slalom; 4. ping-pong